P9-CQZ-691

TEN
STRATEGIES
for Preaching in a
Multi Media Culture

TEN
STRATEGIES
for Preaching in a
Multi Media Culture

THOMAS H. TROEGER

ABINGDON PRESS
Nashville

TEN STRATEGIES FOR PREACHING IN A MULTI MEDIA CULTURE

Copyright © 1996 by Abingdon Press

This book is printed on acid-free, recycled paper.

Library of Congress Cataloging-in-Publication Data

Troeger, Thomas H., 1945–
    Ten strategies for preaching in a multi media culture/Thomas H. Troeger.
        p.   cm.
    Includes bibliographical references.
    ISBN 0-687-00701-1 (pbk.: alk. paper)
        1. Preaching.   2. Mass media—Religious aspects—Christianity.
    I. Title.
    BV4211.2.T7655   1996
    251'.07—dc20   95-44510
                                                                                          CIP

Scripture quotations are from the New Revised Standard Version Bible, copyright © 1989, by the Division of Christian Education of the National Council of the Churches of Christ in the United States of America. Used by permission.

"Noah Built the Ark" is from GOD'S TROMBONES by James Weldon Johnson. Copyright 1927 The Viking Press, Inc., renewed © 1955 by Grace Nail Johnson. Used by permission of Viking Penguin, a division of Penguin Books USA Inc.

96 97 98 99 00 01 02 03 04 05—10 9 8 7 6 5 4 3 2 1

MANUFACTURED IN THE UNITED STATES OF AMERICA

Contents

113975

Contents

In the Path of the Storm

Alert to the Wind

When I was a boy, my father built a small sailboat from a kit. The hull was only a quarter of an inch thick and there were no decks. It was a very light craft, and it would take off like a jack rabbit at the smallest puff of wind. Sometimes the wind would fall completely still, and we were becalmed in the center of the lake. Whenever this happened, my father continued scanning the smooth mirror surface of the water. He would look to see if there were any ruffled shadows of wave, the sure sign that wind is blowing somewhere on the lake. As soon as he saw the darkening water, he would start tracking its path, and he would tell me how much to push out or pull in the boom, and where to sit in the boat so that it would be tilted at the right angle to take maximum advantage of the wind when it hit the sails.

My father could not compel the wind to blow any more than we preachers can conjure up the Holy Spirit to enliven our sermons. But like good sailors, we can use our skill to get ready for the wind, we can formulate strategies for preaching that open us and our congregations to the Spirit.

The word "strategy" suggests a highly controlled activity, the conscious design and implementation of a plan, such as drawing a blueprint or developing a game plan for an athletic competition. There is a similar element of calculation in preparing any sermon:

Where to start?
How to develop it?
Where to end?

But because preaching gives witness to God, our strategies find their deepest origins not in human calculation but in prayer. The finest eloquence, the cleverest presentation, the liveliest and most up-to-date form of communication will only bear fruit if the Spirit is present.

So before we continue with more words about our task, it is wise to remember that the holy realities we name with our lips are greater than our speech. Bernard of Clairvaux put this powerfully in the twelfth century: "Prepare not your ear but your soul; for it is grace that teaches it and not language."[1]

The Path of the Storm

Any preaching strategy worthy of the gospel will combine, then, two elements: an openness to the Spirit *and* the strenuous work of human thought and creation. To hold these together is no easy task, as the history of the presentation of God's word makes clear.

Notice: I do not say simply the history of sermons or the history of preaching. Although this is a book about preaching sermons in congregations, the terms "preaching" and "sermons" may be too confining for a multimedia culture characterized by multiple forms of communication. The terms may imply a single style of communication, a minister in a pulpit delivering the exposition of a biblical text, when we need to consider many methods.

The history of human beings presenting the word of God reveals a multiplicity of strategies, many of them involving a complex relationship between the Holy Spirit, faith, and culture. When we consider what kinds of strategies we need for presenting God's word to a multimedia culture, we are carrying on the tradition of our ancestors who adapted the expression of faith to the popular song and new technologies of their day. Far from rejecting the Bible, we are becoming more biblical by employing the creative interpretative process which runs through scripture and the history of the church.

We can trace that process as the path of a storm, as the witness left by the blowing of the Spirit. Then we can draw from that witness the courage to formulate new strategies for preaching to a multimedia age.

Two Maps of the Past

Here are two maps of the path of the storm to help us find our way in the present. The first is like the map from a world atlas: no local roads or small settlements but the great continental features. The second is more like the map in a tourist guide: not every detail but several of the main sights.

The first map is a hymn about the spreading of the gospel. It shows that the church from its earliest beginnings was deeply related to the world in order to transform the world for the purposes of God.

> The Christians traveled Caesar's roads,
> and as the Spirit led,
> they stopped to carry strangers' loads
> and share their faith and bread.
> By simple acts the word was sown
> and spread from place to place
> till highways of the Roman throne
> became a web of grace.
>
> Then past the reach of Caesar's Rome,
> cross deserts, mountains, ice,
> the word moved on and found a home
> in all who welcomed Christ.
> They carved in stone and traced in glass
> the stories they received
> to help their children's children grasp

the gospel they believed.
But hallowed walls could not contain
the Spirit's growing storm,
the wind whose gathered force ordained
the church's full reform
and sent the word around the globe
to kindle and ignite
new fires of faith to warm and robe
the world in greater light.

The word that traveled Caesar's roads
and raised cathedral spires
still calls to us and lifts our loads
and stirs the Spirit's fires,
and gives us daily cause for praise
and sends us from this place
directing us to seek new ways
to weave a web of grace.[2]

What the hymn paints in a few broad strokes, we now turn to consider in more detail, going back even farther than Caesar to the community of faith in the Hebrew Scriptures.

Consider the psalms. Many of those beloved ancient words had their origins in the surrounding culture. Psalm 29, for example, "is often viewed by modern students as an ancient Canaanite poem written originally to the storm god, Baal, and adapted by Israel with the necessary change in the divine name and other alterations."[3]

The psalm reveals the essential role of the imagination in devising new strategies to present the word of God. It took a lively imagination to see the possibilities for giving witness to Yahweh through words associated with Baal, for adapting a popular song in ways that deepen and enrich the faith of Israel. Although the church has often held that imagination and the Holy Spirit are in conflict, the study of scripture reveals that contrast to be simplistic. The biblical writers themselves display vivid imaginations through which the

Holy Spirit works to create new strategies for presenting the word of God. Thus the author of Luke-Acts did not set out to write history in the modern sense of the term, but instead followed the practice of his contemporaries:

> Ancient histories exhibit an astonishing freedom with traditions and sources. Historical accuracy mattered less than entertainment, plausibility, and persuasiveness. These histories typically promoted particular religious, political, or philosophical objectives. The author of Luke-Acts apparently sought to refashion the literature and traditions of the church into a triumphant narrative capable of providing the church with a heritage and an identity compatible with life in cities of the Roman Empire.[4]

Likewise, Mark was an imaginative evangelist who was not constrained by "historical accuracy" but who developed a form of proclamation to which no previous document

> exactly conforms with its literary properties. Its themes of travel, conflict with supernatural foes, suffering, and secrecy resonate with Homer's *Odyssey* and Greek romantic novels. Its focus on the character identity, and death of a single individual reminds one of ancient biographies. Its dialogues, tragic outcome, and peculiar ending call to mind Greek drama. Some have suggested that *the author created a new, mixed genre for narrating the life and death of Jesus.*[5]

To create a "new mixed genre" or to write a history whose primary mode is not historical accuracy but "entertainment, plausibility, and persuasiveness" is to devise a new strategy for presenting the word of God in a highly imaginative way. The same is true of the early Christians who

> wrote letters in the names of others, a widespread ancient literary practice called "pseudepigrapha" (meaning "false attribution"). In some cases, authors wrote in the name of an

apostle in order to enable the deceased hero to speak to conditions relevant to churches of a later date.[6]

These literary practices of the biblical writers reveal that the communication of the gospel early on involved a variety of different strategies.

As we move beyond the time of the biblical writers, we see Christians extending and developing a spectrum of homiletical strategies, ranging from allegorical approaches to more literal readings to poetic interpretations to the use of clear rational categories.[7]

And to name these strategies is to confine ourselves to the interpretation of texts. There were millions of believers through the ages who were not literate but who had a profound faith in Christ and who created or benefited from an astonishing variety of strategies to present the word of God:

> They carved in stone and traced in glass
> the stories they received
> to help their children's children grasp
> the gospel they believed.

The visual arts were so central to the presentation of the gospel in the Middle Ages that they even influenced the ways preachers spoke and gestured!

> Late-medieval preachers were "skilled visual performers" who used a repertoire of gestures known to their audiences from paintings. Manuals of such gestures existed, providing a stylized body language that accompanied and heightened the verbal communication.[8]

This visual homiletic extended to medieval drama and to plays that "were often given as interludes in sermons, composed of material from popular devotional texts and directed by preachers."[9]

In the light of these visual and dramatic homiletics, we see what a radical new strategy it was to print and read the Bible in the vernacular. It involved two important innovations. The first was theological: It took the authority for reading and interpreting the Bible away from the church hierarchy and put it into the hands of the people. The second innovation was technological: the mass reproduction of texts by the printing press. The two innovations went hand in hand, giving a distinctive character to Protestantism that continues to this day:

> Protestantism was born with printing and has been the religion in which printing—the printed Bible, the catechism, newspapers, and journals—has played a vital part. The present crisis in these publications is undoubtedly a sign of a very deep crisis of identity. *How is it possible to be a Protestant in a world in which radio and television are the easiest forms of communication?*[10]

With the most recent innovations in digital technology we can also add, How is it possible to be a Protestant in a world in which three kinds of media are converging (text, audio, and video) into one new mixed genre, multimedia? The question suggests why it is so often difficult for many Protestant ministers and theologians to play freely with different strategies for presenting the word of God: To do so feels like violating our religious core. As the saying goes, "We are people of the Book."

But if we trace the path of the Spirit through the sixteenth century and onward, we encounter multiple ways that the word of God was presented, strategies that went far beyond a constricted biblicism and preaching from the pulpit:

—the spread of popular meditative practices and spiritual disciplines

—the composition of cantatas and oratorios

—giving public witness to Christ such as the testimony of women who converted John Bunyan, the author of *Pilgrim's Progress*

—the rise of hymnody

—the writing of spiritual poetry

—the singing schools that congregational song inspired

—the achievement of African American slaves in fusing together song, dance, testifying, prayer, and preaching in one flowing expression of God's word

—the rituals and music of the civil rights movement

—the participatory Bible study of base communities . . .

Where does the list end? It is too long to record in this brief book. Our task is to make our own contribution to the list, to devise strategies for presenting the word of God to a multimedia culture in ways that are faithful to Christ and the Spirit.

The Audiovisual Cultures of the Media

"Culture" is an elusive word to define. We might say it is the total constellation of stories, symbols, values, and behaviors that characterize the society in which a group of people live. But any single definition does not quite capture the encompassing, fluid, changeable nature of culture. A professional anthropologist said to me, "Culture is to humans as water is to fish."[11] We live in it unaware of its pervasive nature until we find ourselves in another culture and are struck by the strangeness of what we encounter.

The difficulties of defining "culture" are germane to understanding the impact of the media. Studies of how television functions in different societies and social strata reveal that " 'Watching television' cannot be assumed to be a one-dimensional activity of equivalent meaning or significance at all times for all who perform it."[12] Therefore to speak of "multimedia" or "mass media culture" as though it were one monolithic, homogeneous reality is inaccurate. In fact there is a complex interactive relationship between viewers and media. Even the same individual may use the media in a multiplicity of ways, from watching a favorite program with great intensity to leaving on the television or radio to provide background noise, from surfing on channels to browsing on hyperlinks.

While keeping in mind the different ways that the media interact with various cultures and social classes, I am using the phrase "multimedia culture" to refer to the world of "audiovisually oriented people," for whom effective communication is characterized by "the resurgence of the imagination, the importance of affective relationships and values, and the dissolution of national and cultural frontiers."[13] Our task as preachers is to develop new strategies for presenting the gospel to a world that speaks an audiovisual language.

Distortion and Resistance

There are dangers in this work, and there are reasons for resisting the values and methods of the new media. Neil Postman reminds us how the media can distort the discipline that is characteristic of authentic religion:

> Who cares how many boxes of cereal can be sold via television? We need to know if television changes our conception of reality, the relationship of the rich to the poor, the idea of happiness itself. A preacher who confines himself [or herself] to considering how a medium can increase his audience will miss the significant question: In what sense do new media alter what is meant by religion, by church, even by God?[14]

Postman's bracing critique might stop us cold except that there have always been dangers in presenting the word of

God through new media. The Four Gospels of the New Testament are a case in point.

When the evangelists began to set down the stories that had circulated by word of mouth, their work represented a brand new strategy: "Some Christians claimed that they preferred 'the living and abiding voice' (i.e. of oral transmission of Christian teaching) to written documents."[15] We now treasure the Gospels so deeply that this is almost impossible for us to imagine: Christians were opposed to the writing of the New Testament!

Before we dismiss their resistance as an antique curiosity in the church's story, we need to acknowledge that subsequent history has shown that writing down the Gospels did not result in unadulterated good. When the church was born, the entire community, women and men together, took part in presenting the word of God. Writing down the Good News of Christ reduced the story to the author's perspective. Once the text became authoritative, other believers could not offer their version, could not contribute stories and insights that the author had left out or relegated to the margins.

As the text became more and more sacrosanct, it was often used to keep slaves in their place, to silence women, to block the advance of the scientific revolution, to encourage hatred and bigotry. The long and tragic history of the misuse of scripture gives us reason to recall those early Christians who resisted writing the gospel down. They stand as a reminder to us that no strategy for presenting the word of God, even when inspired by the Holy Spirit, can communicate the full and perfect wholeness of the divine.

"Infinite Translatability"

The apostle Paul found theological comfort in the realization that broken and imperfect preaching is a part of our broken and imperfect world: It reminds us "this extraordinary power belongs to God and does not come from us" (2 Cor. 4:7*b*).

Humbled by Paul's insight and the history of misdirected preaching, I have no reason to believe that I am without my own distortions and limitations. I make no claim that the strategies in this book are ideal ways to present the gospel. I offer them encouraging you to try them, modify them, and develop your own. I offer them trusting entirely in the "extraordinary power" that "belongs to God," and believing in the resilience of the gospel that has endured two thousand years of our imperfect attempts to proclaim it. I look at that history and I find hope in the observation that

> if, at this moment before the dawn of a new century, the church in the industrial nations is confused, not knowing what to do with its inheritance, this is because it cannot yet see clearly the new cultural milieu into which it is already moving. If Andrew Walls is right, however, the church can take heart from the evidence that each time the cultural base of the Christian religion was about to crumble, Christianity has been saved by its diffusion into a new milieu. And if what Walls calls Christianity's *"infinite translatability"* disturbs the guardians of orthodoxy, let them also find reassurance from this history. For it shows that, whatever undreamt of forms the faith has evolved in each new phase, the dominant themes of former times have been added to rather than lost.[16]

When preachers develop new strategies for presenting the word of God, they are giving witness to the "infinite translatability" of Christianity. They are not abandoning faith in Christ but carrying on the dynamic tradition of the church, which for all its failures and injustices, has still managed to hand on the Good News of the Savior from generation to generation.

A World in a Grain of Sand

The "infinite translatability" of Christianity may seem a rather grand concept for the sermons that preachers prepare and deliver week after week. A sermon appears to be no more than a grain of sand in the vast shifting landscape of faith and culture. But as the poet reminds us, it is possible "to see a world in a Grain of Sand,"[17] and that is also true of sermons.

In an era when grains of sand are transformed into silicon chips or into microcircuits of glass optical fibers that connect the entire world, we anticipate that it is time for new strategies. Each time we use a new strategy in presenting the word of God we are involved with something greater than homiletical tinkering. We are suggesting a world of meaning, a theological universe with important implications for our understanding of God and humanity and the relationship between them.

For instance, all of the sermons in this book are written in the style of oral and aural speech.

Like this.
Not the long sentences of written prose.
But brief sentences.
Words and clauses.
Each one getting a line.
This is the way we talk.
The way we listen.
The way we hear.
Now and then preachers can get away with longer and more complex sentences that feature relative clauses that go on for quite a while, such as the one you are reading at this moment.
But.
That's for the eye.
Not the ear.
It makes for hard listening.
And it often makes for congregations getting lost.
Short lines
are easier to follow.

Clear delivery is more than method.
Clear delivery is a theological issue:
How accessible is God?
Tangled language
becomes tangled revelation,
an obstacle course
for the congregation,
for the heart hungering for God.
Remember:
you can see a world
in a grain of sand,
you can see a world
in a sermon.

The Theological Significance of New Strategies

Every strategy we employ for presenting the word of God has theological import. If we use only stories, we suggest that God is not revealed through reason, even though our minds are a gift from God. If we use only concepts, we suggest that God is not revealed through emotion, even though our hearts are a gift from God. Therefore, we need many strategies to suggest what we can never fully capture: the multitude of different ways that God comes to us. We use all that we are to give witness to all that God is. In doing this we are more faithful to the wholeness of God, and we increase our capacity to engage people with the gospel, especially generations who have grown up with mass media and now converging multimedia that appeal to them through multiple levels of sense and meaning.

Of course, new strategies for presenting the word of God could result in manipulative preaching, by reducing proclamation to what is attractive and entertaining. But it does not have to be that way. Just as theologians have developed critical criteria for assessing claims of truth and right doctrine, we can do the same in considering new strategies for preaching. Pierre Babin names some helpful ways to test our new forms of communication that include: checking our perceptions and re-sponses with others, examining them in the light of history, and evaluating the fruits of what we have done.[18]

These criteria can also help preachers to make a balanced judgment about the media. For the church needs to avoid the self-righteous tone that often comes with vilifying the media. Despite their limitations, the media also do good. I think of people who sought out medical care or family counseling because of television programs that reached them when nothing else did. I think of others who, while surfing the internet for fast-breaking news, have been moved to provide relief for those suffering from natural disasters, and I think of people who have become more environmentally sensitive because of visual images of the earth taken from outer space. We sometimes forget these things when we intone the litany of media abuses: the crass commercialism, the bias, the vio-lence, the gratuitous sex. The media, like most human en-deavors, represent neither pure good nor pure evil.

One benefit of employing the imaginative methods of the media for presenting the word of God is that such strategies, provided they are faithful to Christ, can help people develop a greater sense of discernment: What images are being used to sell us what we do not need? What images are calling us to ministry in the world?

The Alchemy of Grace

We gain courage to develop new strategies for preaching by recalling that the gospel took increasing root in the ancient world because Christians mastered the most effective means of communication in their day: classical rhetoric, the system-atic art of public persuasion that the Greeks and Romans employed in their political and communal gatherings. Al-though believers often contrasted their preaching with what they considered to be "pagan," a close analysis reveals that "the seemingly alternative rhetorics, the classical or pagan and the Christian, were more nearly one than their respective practitioners, interested in scoring off each other, would have us believe."[19]

The church did not spread the news of God's redeeming work in the world by isolating itself from the surrounding culture:

> Christians, the quintessential outsiders as they appeared to men like Nero, Pliny, Tacitus, and Suetonius, talked and wrote themselves into a position where they spoke and wrote the rhetoric of empire. For it is perfectly certain that had they not been able to do this, Constantine or no Constantine, Christianity would never have become a world religion.[20]

The church's creative use of the arts that the world supplied did not stop with the verbal arts of oratory and writing. As new technologies developed through the centuries, believers saw yet other ways to draw people toward the transforming grace of God:

> Many of the cathedrals on the way to Compostela and the Shrine of Saint James were built by architects who were alchemists. They wanted pilgrims to enter their cathedrals as if they were going into the alchemist's egg, to be transformed from their old selves into new ones.[21]

Transforming people "from their old selves into new ones" is the work of Christ. But it is a noble and holy aspiration to plan a cathedral or a life of preaching that would be a vessel for that transformation. This, then, is the ultimate goal of new strategies for preaching: to use the full range of the gifts of human communication as a medium for the alchemy of grace, for the transformative work of the Spirit that makes us new creations in Christ.

STRATEGY 1

Assume There Is More to the Story

Our first new strategy reminds us that what we call "new" seldom is. It usually means "new to us," and that is the case here. By imagining that there is more to a biblical story than what we find in the text, we practice an ancient way of interpreting the gospel to people living in different times and places.

For example, homilies in the Eastern church from the fifth to the ninth century "testify to the power of an imaginative world at which the New Testament itself does no more than hint, but which in practice formed the real world of Christian belief."[1] Although I do not suggest that we return to the same elaboration that marked those Byzantine sermons, I believe that there are principles that can guide our extended imagining of biblical stories so that what we present strengthens our understanding of the spirit of the text.

I find these principles at work in a charming medieval expansion of the story of the Magi from the Gospel of Matthew. *The Story of the Three Kings*[2] takes liberties with the biblical text and reaches beyond Matthew's narrative to what happens with the Magi when they travel home, the shrines they establish, their death and the conflicted history over who will keep their revered corpses. And yet for all of this elaboration, the spirit of the gospel keeps breaking through in fresh ways.

John of Hildesheim conflates the gospels and portrays the Magi meeting the shepherds on their way to Christ. The shepherds share all that they have seen and heard, "And when these three glorious kings had spoken to these shepherds and had given them great gifts, they rode forth on their way."[3] That little scene may be entirely apocryphal, but it expresses the gospel: the way the birth of Christ awakens our hospitality not only to the child who is born, but to others as well.

John of Hildesheim also portrays the Magi as coming from different lands, but meeting together on a "highway beside the hill of Calvary."[4] After their visit to the child, although "they departed from each other in their bodily persons, they never did so in their hearts."[5] John plays freely with the details, but he gets the gospel right: Hospitality, redemption, and the communion of believers shine forth in his story and draw us to Christ as surely as the star drew the Magi.

That was in the fourteenth century, but in our own century there is a splendid example of the same strategy, imagining there is more to the story in a way that deepens and extends the spirit of the biblical narrative. James Weldon Johnson's *God's Trombones* captures in poetry the grandeur and freedom of generations of African American preaching, elaborating upon the biblical text to bring us closer to the Spirit that breathes through the words of scripture. In the following example the exaggeration and color of the language evoke the affective dimensions of belief, the way faith can look absurd to a skeptical world, and the tenacity of a heart set on God:

And Noah commenced to work on the ark.
And he worked for about one hundred years.
And ev'ry day the crowd came round
To make fun of Old Man Noah.
And they laughed and they said: Tell us, old man,
Where do you expect to sail that boat
Up here amongst the hills?

But Noah kept on a-working.
And ev'ry once in a while Old Noah would stop,

> He'd lay down his hammer and lay down his saw,
> And take his staff in hand;
> And with his long, white beard a-flying in the wind,
> And the gospel light a-gleaming from his eye,
> Old Noah would preach God's word:
> Sinners, oh, sinners,
> Repent, for the judgment is at hand . . .[6]

At their best, extension and elaboration of the biblical story are not flights of pure fancy. They are theologically disciplined acts of imagination that seek to honor the spirit of the text while they draw upon the larger perspectives of the whole gospel, upon the tradition and experience of the church that extends throughout Christian history.

Here is an example of my own in which I imagine that there is more to the story of the wedding at Cana than John recorded. Since a wedding marks a beginning and not an ending, it seems only natural to wonder about scenes from the marriage that followed the nuptial celebration.

Scenes from a Marriage

John 2:1-11

I would like to think there was some wine left over.
Jesus supplied enough.
John tells us
"there were six stone water jars . . .
each holding twenty or thirty gallons."
If three jars held twenty gallons,
three times twenty is sixty.
And if three jars held thirty,
three times thirty is ninety.
And sixty gallons plus ninety gallons
equals one hundred fifty gallons.
One hundred fifty gallons!

That is a lot of wine to drink.
Especially since they had already polished off
the initial supply.
Surely, one twenty-gallon jar would have sufficed.
But no.
Jesus is extravagant,
wildly extravagant.
It is not unreasonable to believe some wine was left.
And I would like to think
that when the celebration was over
and the couple had left for their honeymoon
and the guests had departed,
that some friend or family member of the couple,
poured the wine that remained into smaller containers
and corked them,
and when the couple returned,
presented them with several crates of the splendid wine.
"Here, this is the wine the rabbi from Nazareth supplied.
I thought you might like to have it for special occasions."

I picture the couple delighted,
smiling to think that on the meager budget of newlyweds
they can enjoy such a heavenly vintage
with their low-cost suppers.
In the way of eager young couples,
they do not plan very well at first
so that at the end of two or three years,
they realize,
extravagant as Jesus was,
they will some day run out.
So they begin to save the wine for special occasions,
bringing it out
on their anniversary,
on the birth and dedication of a child,
at family reunions,
on high holy days

that feature feasting and drinking.
And every time they taste the wine,
they relive their wedding day,
and they recall how at the first sip
of Jesus' wine
they had looked at each other
with eyes that shone with a love
whose intensity caught even them by surprise.

And so the years pass
until they are an old couple,
keenly aware that "all flesh is grass,"
springing up in youth,
then quickly fading.
I picture the old couple on a chilly night.
She is in front of the fire,
trying to warm her feet and hands
for they are always cold now.
He pauses coming into the room
where she sits on a bench pulled right up to the grate.
He studies her in the light of the fire:
the shape of her forehead,
the deep creases in her face,
and the lips he has kissed ten thousand times.
All of a sudden,
with a prompting he cannot explain,
he blurts out:
"Honey?"
At first she does not hear him
so he calls again,
"Honey?"
She slowly looks up, and he says,
"Honey, what if we finish the wine tonight.
The rabbi's wine.
There's just one little bottle left.
It might warm you up some."

"Sure, sure," she says,
"that would be good."
So he goes and gets the wine and brings it back to the fire
with the only clean chalice he can find.
He sets it down and uncorks the wine speculating:
"I wonder if it will still be good,
after all these years."
"Always has been," she says.
"The rabbi's wine has never gone bad,
it's as amazing as the way he provided it."
The husband pours the first serving
and hands his wife the chalice.
She sips and hands it to him.
They look at each other and nod their agreement:
the wine is as rich as the day they were married.

They drink very slowly,
and as they drink they start to tell stories.
She says:
"I remember when Sarah was born.
You would have thought
nobody had ever been a father before,
the way you carried on,
calling in the whole neighborhood,
they consumed an entire crate of this wine,
as if it were our wedding all over again."
"Well, you did just about the same,
when Benjamin and Rebecca
brought home our first grandchild."
The wife laughs a hearty laugh,
"Yeah, I did didn't I?
Oh, those were such good times,
good enough to want them never to stop."

He pours some more wine,
and they each take a sip

and he stirs the fire,
and they sit absorbed in the flame.
She sees him out of the corner of her eye
and notices he is trying to hold back tears.
She knows what he is thinking:
He is remembering when the third child died.
Been terribly sick.
Tried everything.
But he died anyway.
All she could pray for weeks on end was
"My God, my God why have you forsaken us?"
They were both so distraught,
and God didn't seem to answer,
they didn't know what to do but blame the other one.
One evening he came home
and she had supper ready,
and they set things out on the table
without saying a single word,
going through motions
that had become rituals of habit,
the only thing holding them together
day by day now.
When they sat down they realized
she had not gotten water from the well
and he had not brought home any wine from market.
So he got up
and found one of the bottles of wine from their wedding.
Might as well open it now.
No sense saving it for special occasions anymore.
So he opened it and poured some wine for each of them.
And when the wine touched their lips
they tasted grace in their hearts,
and they broke down and sobbed together.
The grief of their loss never went away
—how could it—
but the strength to carry the grief together

that was what the wine of Jesus gave them.
And now sitting in front of the fire,
he turns to look at her,
and hearing him move
she turns toward him
and they look at each other,
and she takes his hand saying,
"Yes, Honey, I know, I know."
He is silent,
then holds the bottle upside down over the chalice.
There are a few last drops.
He hands the chalice to her:
"Here you finish it."
She takes the smallest sip
and hands it back to him
pointing out there is still the tiniest bit at the bottom.
He puts the brim to his lips
and throws back his head
holding the chalice straight over him,
then slowly brings it down
and holds it between them.
"That's it," he says
with a voice that sounds both satisfied and sad.
"All gone.
None to pass on to the children
or the grandchildren now.
Just the story
of our wedding at Cana,
and the rabbi who blessed us with wine.
Just the story.
But no wine."
"Not to worry" responds his wife.
"Not to worry.
As long as people come to his table,
there will be more."

STRATEGY 2
Create a Parable

One of the greatest obstacles to receiving the word of God is how cluttered our hearts and heads are. We are stuffed to capacity with our habitual ways of thinking and responding. This represents a stiff challenge for preaching. How do we create enough free space inside people that they can entertain looking at the world in light of the gospel and the reign of God? Direct argument seldom works, because it feels like an intrusive guest telling us how to rearrange the furniture in our mental house. We resent it, and we resist.

But a story that engages our imagination in order to awaken the deeper resonances of our lives is less immediately threatening. Parables entice us to consider: What if the world does not operate the way we assume it does? Since a parable is only a story, we may be willing to go along, to play with possibilities for which our cluttered minds usually have no room. The imaginative character of the story liberates us from our usual patterns of perception and response. Thus Jesus' parables free us to consider the astonishing God who turns the calculations of human judgment upside down.

I wrote the following parable for the consecration Sunday of a church that had chosen as its stewardship theme, "The Grateful Heart." As in the case of our first strategy, "imagining there is more to the story," I develop the parable by expanding upon scripture. But unlike "Scenes from a Marriage," this presentation of God's word involves six preachers: a narrator in the pulpit, and five pantomimists. I have kept the action simple so that even those without dramatic training can, after adequate rehearsal, present the story with confidence.

Although the script gives the chief role to a woman, the part can be filled by either a woman or a man, depending on who your most capable pantomimist is.

The church where I led this had a gifted pianist who added appropriate background music at various dramatic moments: fluttering music when the moth appeared, stormy music when it rained, menacing music when the thief broke in. This was a fine touch, but it is not necessary if you lack the musical resources.

One last direction: Keep it simple. Do not use any more props or costumes than suggested. Part of why something like this works is its spareness, the room it allows for the imagination of the congregation. If the front of the church is cluttered or costumes are elaborate, you will leave less space for the creative energies of grace to enter people's hearts and minds.

The Grateful Heart

Matthew 6:19-21

The narrator reads the story, often slowing down or stopping altogether to allow the pantomimists to act things out. Single-word lines indicate very slow, drawn-out phrases.

Once upon a time there was a fabulously wealthy woman.
She had a vast treasure in gold coins,
and thousand-dollar bills.
She would carry her treasure with her wherever she went.

A character in dance tights comes down the aisle with her treasure box, puts it on a table up front, and counts her imaginary coins and bills.

And when she found what looked like a safe place,
she would put down her treasure box
and count
every
last
coin
and
every
last
bill
with glee
and
with great fear
that someone might steal it.
The woman decided that she needed a safe place
to store her vast treasure.
So she looked around her house
and decided that since her house
was on a high hill
and had thick walls
and had plenty of guard dogs,
it would be safe to store the treasure
underneath her bed.

The character takes the treasure box and begins to store it beneath the table.

But as she bent down to tuck the treasure safely away,
she felt she was not only hiding her wealth,
she was stowing away her heart as well.

The character straightens up and takes out of her shirt and unfolds a large paper heart in bright red, perfectly shaped like a valentine heart. Then she carefully refolds the heart and puts it in the treasure box and places the box beneath the table and walks away in a confident manner.

She was certain

the treasure was safe and sound now.
But while she was away
a moth came flying over the heads of the guard dogs
and through the windows of the thick walls
of the woman's house,
and found the treasure under the bed.

Another character comes down the aisle, in another color of dance tights, and flapping arms like wings. The moth flutters around the treasure chest, bends down to it, and comes back up making dramatic chewing actions, and then flutters off.

That night
before the woman went to bed
she decided that she would entertain herself
counting her treasure.
She came into the room
and opened the treasure chest
only to discover that there were holes
in the dollar bills.
And when she held up her heart
it looked like this:

The woman unfolds her heart [actually another heart that has been planted in the treasure chest ahead of time] and there are moth holes in it, including chomps taken out of the edges. She puts on an expression of utter discouragement at losing some of her treasure and her heart.

Part of her treasure had flown out the window with the moth.
And part of her heart had disappeared as well,
for where your treasure is
there will your heart be also.
The woman decided she would lose no more of her treasure.
And no more of her heart either.
So even though it was late at night,
she hefted the treasure box
and walked up to a tiny room

in the attic where there was not a single window
and only a dull lamp to provide a little light.
She thought to herself:
"No moth will ever get in here."
And she refolded her heart
and she put it in the treasure chest,
and went to bed that night
certain that her treasure and her heart
were as safe and as sound as they could ever be.

All of the above actions are enacted by the woman as the narrator reads slowly. Then the woman sits down out of sight as the narrator continues.

During the night
a great storm came up.
There was strong wind,
and fierce lightning
and loud thunderclaps
and a drenching rain.
But the woman slept through it all,
certain that her treasure was safe and sound.
But what she did not know
was that there was a leak
in the roof over the attic room
and water began to pour in
and land on her treasure.

Another character in blue dance tights comes in with a large watering can and standing directly over the treasure pretends to hold the can as if it had a limitless supply of water to pour out.

The next morning the woman awoke to a sunny day.
But before she went out to enjoy the fresh air,
she went upstairs to the little attic room.
As she entered she could smell the dampness
of everything in the room.
In a panic she opened her treasure box
and discovered that the thousand-dollar bills

bore rust marks
from the soaked treasure box.
And when she picked up her heart
it looked like this.

Again the woman enacts the actions as the narrator speaks. This time the heart has the same moth-eaten patterns as before but in addition it has patterns of orange-reddish rust.

Her treasure was decaying
and her heart as well.
For where your treasure is,
there will your heart be also.
Now the woman decided that the only thing to do
was to have a safe built into
the thickest and hardest wall in her great house.
So that day, instead of enjoying the sun,
she hired a workman to build
a big strong safe with
a fancy lock
whose combination would be known only to her.
Then she placed her treasure
and her heart back in the treasure box
and put it all in the safe,
shut the door
and whirled the combination
this way and that
and pulled on the safe handle
to make sure it was locked safe and sound.

The woman enacts the actions of placing the treasure in the safe and locking it and then sits down out of sight. Next a character in gray dance tights, with a gray gunnysack over his shoulder and a gray eye mask mimes the robbery which the narrator describes below.

Then the woman went to bed
and slept more soundly than ever before.

But during the night a clever thief
fed porterhouse steaks to the guard dogs
and found an unlocked window on the ground floor.
He sneaked quietly into the great room
and found the safe built into the wall.
He put his ear next to the lock
and began slowly and meticulously
to turn the lock,
listening
for
the sound
of the tumblers.
Now he was a very experienced thief
and his ears were very sensitive to the sounds
of combination locks.
And he found the right combination
and he took out the treasure box
and he filled his bags with what he found.
Then he put the box back in the safe
and shut the door
and left.
The next morning the woman
came downstairs and decided to count her treasure.
She opened the safe
and took out the box
and lifted the lid
and fainted.
When she came to,
she discovered that the thief had missed one little coin
hidden in the shadow of a corner of the box
and next to the coin
she discovered what was left of her heart.

The woman holds up one coin and one little piece of heart, recognizable as just the tip.

The thief had taken the rest of the treasure away

and the rest of the woman's heart as well.
For where your treasure is
there will your heart be also.
She was so sad that she walked out of the house
and down toward the village.
And as she walked she met a man
begging by the side of the road.
He needed food for his children.
Even the smallest coin would be
a great gift in his eyes.
She looked at the man.
Then she looked at her last coin
and the little piece of heart that she had left,
and she thought
"Why not give them away?
I have tried every other way
to preserve my treasure and my heart
and none of them has worked."
So she dropped the coin in the man's tin cup
and gave him also
what was left of her heart.
The man shook her hand in gratitude
and the two of them went their separate ways.

All of the above actions are enacted. The beggar can be in dance tights the same color as those of the woman. He carries a tin cup so that when she drops the coin in the cup we hear it clink. Then both walk down separate aisles toward the back of the church. But they return as the story continues.

Now many years passed
and we do not know much about
what happened to the woman.
But one day she was walking along
the street when she saw someone
who reminded her of the man
to whom she had given her last coin.

She was not certain if it was the same person.
This time the man carried a briefcase,
and his face shone with confidence.
But the man identified the woman right away.
He stopped her and told the story of how
her single coin had helped his family buy just
enough food to survive
until he got a job.
He told how his children had grown up
strong and healthy
and how all these years
he had dreamed of someday repaying
the woman who had given her last coin to him.
And with that he reached into his briefcase
and unfolded
a heart that was full
and bright
and healthy.
And as he handed it to her
he said to her:
Where your treasure is,
there will your heart be also.

All of the above is enacted by the man in the same tights as before but this time with a briefcase instead of a tin cup. The woman holds up the heart for all to see, and the congregation sings a happy hymn of thanksgiving or the choir an anthem of great joy, while the players return down the aisles.

If the sermon is presented on consecration or stewardship Sunday, then each person may be handed a bright heart upon bringing a pledge forward.

STRATEGY 3
Play with an Image

Despite historical debates about images in church, the use of the eye in worship has never disappeared. Even in churches that have Reformed roots there is a visual manifestation of their iconoclastic theology: for example, the clear glass windows and plain interiors of New England meetinghouses. In leaving behind one form of visual statement another is created.

If there is an absence of adequate visual stimulation in the church, then the need may take other forms in the larger society. As Gregor Goethals observes,

> The arts we generally call "popular," like television, have taken over a major role that visual images historically performed: the public communication of shared beliefs. Like traditional religious art, the mass media present symbols of authority and portray common values. In both high and popular culture artists construct visual meanings, attempting in various ways to render visible invisible truths which illuminate experience. In contemporary society this impulse has found extensive expression outside the church.[1]

Whether the images of multimedia work for good or ill—and they have the capacity to do either—they all share in common a transitory character that eclipses the longer historical perspective that comes with a religious tradition. The media

may serve as agents and mechanisms for our historical am-
nesia as they systematically relegate recent historical experience into the past. Disasters, both natural and human, the rise
and fall of regimes, crucial events that seem for a moment to
define or destroy a people—all seem to be daily wiped away
from memory. Few seem to care about prolonged memories
or sustained questions about the present and future.[2]

Since people are not going to stop watching television, or
playing computer games, we need a fruitful preaching strategy
for making the enduring images and prolonged memories of
tradition vividly engaging. If we are successful, our congregations will find that the Bible and church tradition offer a critical
perspective for viewing the images of the media, even when
that is not the explicit point of our preaching.

I offer now a sermon that plays with a biblical image in a
creative way. I assume that this one sermon is not the only
time the text will be presented. Unlike the media, the church
returns again and again to the core passages and images of
our faith. Playing with the image in this sermon may help
people come back to other dimensions in the biblical passage
when it is the text of a more conventional sermon.

This sermon calls for two actors and a narrator. It also
requires as its only prop approximately twenty to twenty-five
cardboard boxes, in sizes that are available from moving com-
panies. You will need to have covered the boxes with spray
paint or colored paper. Also, be sure their tops and bottoms are
taped level so they will sit securely on the chancel floor and on
top of one another. When the skit begins, half the boxes are on
each side of the front of the church, out of view if possible.

The Dividing Wall

Ephesians 2:11-22[3]

*A man and woman walk back and forth in front of the church,
initially holding hands.*

Woman: I like this garden. I like it a lot.
Man: Oh, it's a splendid garden, a beautiful garden, the perfect garden.

They drop hands, and move about pretending to smell the flowers, pick fruit, and examine plants.

Man: You know, though, it would look better if we had some marigolds over here.
Woman: Marigolds? No. I don't think so. What do you want to do that for. You just said it's a perfect garden.
Man: Well, it's not quite perfect enough. I think I'll just put a row of orange and gold marigolds right here.

She begins to march off a line that is at right angles to the congregation so that it looks to them as though she is dividing the front of the church in two halves, hers on the one side, his on the other. He meanwhile gets ready to plant some imaginary marigolds. But she stands in his way with her arms crossed.

Woman: You don't plant them any farther than this.
Man: Why not?
Woman: Because this side is my side.
Man: What do you mean *my* side?
Woman: You know, "my," as in I, me, my, mine.
Man: No, I don't know. What do you mean [mimicking her inflection] "My as in I, me, my, mine?"
Woman: Here, I'll show you.

The woman goes and gets the first "brick" [box], handling it as if it really were a great, heavy rock, putting it dramatically down in front of the man.

Everything from here over is not for marigolds, orange or yellow or gold. No marigolds. This is mine.

While the man plants marigolds with his back turned to the woman, she slips over onto his side of the boundary, which is now marked by the first brick.

Man:　　　What do you think you're doing?
Woman:　　I like the shade of this tree.
Man:　　　Well, it is not your tree to enjoy.
Woman:　　I have always enjoyed this tree. It is my favorite shade tree.
Man:　　　It is not your tree at all. It is *my* tree.

As the man goes and gets a "brick" and puts it next to the original one, he mimics the woman's original declaration, only slower and more forcefully.

> You know *my* as in I, me, my, mine. My marigolds, yellow and orange and gold, and my shade tree.

The woman looks disgusted, out toward the congregation. While she is looking in silence, the man crosses in front of her and picks up some soil from her side of the wall. The woman speaks just as the man is rising with soil in cupped hands.

Woman:　　And what do you think you are doing with that topsoil?
Man:　　　It is for my marigolds.
Woman:　　They may be your marigolds, but it is my soil. Put it back.

The man hesitates, the woman clinches her fist. The man drops the soil, and the woman goes to get the next brick. While the woman is away, the man grabs some soil and runs back to the marigolds. Returning with the brick, the woman looks down at the place where the soil was removed, and the man whistles and looks impishly like nothing has happened.

Woman:　　I don't like the sound of your whistle.

The woman goes and gets two more bricks and puts them beside the others so that now there is a row of them side by side at right angles to the congregation and clearly dividing the front of the church in two halves. The woman puts a foot on top of this first row of bricks and looks imperiously down upon the man planting marigolds. He goes and gets another brick and starts the second row of the wall, placing the brick on the woman's foot with a vengeance.

Woman: Ow! Watch it. That's *my* foot.

Man: It may be your foot. But this is my land and I don't like your shadow on my property.

The man goes back for yet another brick, now slowing down the action and beginning to look sad and burdened by the work of hauling the bricks.

Narrator: Generations passed and everyone was born on one side of the wall or the other. Since the wall had been there for as long as anyone could remember, they all assumed that it would be there forever. And whenever they were discontent with their lives they always blamed the person on the other side of the wall and that only built it higher.

The man and woman put up a new brick with every statement they make.

Woman: I don't like the way you get all the morning light.

Man: I don't like the way you get all the evening light.

Woman: You look strange to me.

Man: We don't associate with people of your kind.

Woman: That's a man for you.

Man: Oh, that's a woman for you.

Woman: Look at that beautiful fruit tree.

She looks toward the other side of the wall, standing on tiptoe and reaching to pick fruit while the man brings a brick.

Man: I, me, my, mine. *[Then he reaches over the wall toward the ground on the woman's side.]* If I could just divert this stream to water my great shade tree.

Woman
[bringing
a brick]:   I, me, my, mine.

When this brick is in place, each stands pointing toward the person on the other side and they speak in unison.

Woman
and   If I could just kill him (her) and take over the
Man   other side of the wall, my heart would not be
together: restless and I would be at peace.

Narrator: And still more generations passed and everyone
                  who was born was born on one side of the wall
                  or the other. And the wall had now been there
                  so long that people began to believe it was God
                  who had built the wall, and so they strengthened
                  the wall and built it yet higher in the name of
                  religion.

The man and woman continue to put up a new brick with every statement they make.

Man   Why do you pray like that? Have you not read
[with hands   that our ancestors raised their hands to the
raised]:   heavens?
Woman
[on knees
with hands   Why do you pray like that? Have you not read
clasped]:   that every knee is to bow to God?

Man: Mine is the true worship.
Woman: Mine is the true worship.

The woman and man, now silent, continue to build the wall while the narrator speaks slowly and deliberately, sometimes pausing to observe them at their work.

Narrator: And so it went from generation to generation, people making the wall higher and higher, stronger and stronger, sometimes knowing why and sometimes just doing it out of fear and ignorance.

The narrator waits for the wall to be completed. It should be tall enough that neither the woman nor the man can see over it. In rehearsing the sermon, it is important to figure out just how the boxes will go on top of one another so that the wall does not tumble.

Narrator: New generations came along, and there the wall stood and would have stood forever, except one day someone called out:

Man: Helloooooo. Helloooo. Is anybody over there?

Woman: Yes, I am.

Man: Well, this wall is so high, it is blocking out the sunlight, and my yellow and orange and gold marigolds are not growing well.

Woman: What marigolds?

Man: Oh, you can't see them. That's what I mean: This wall is too high. Let's take it down.

Woman *[panic in her face]:* Take down the wall? I can't even see you. How do I know you won't do something awful? This wall stays until I can see you.

The man tries jumping. But the wall is too high.

Woman: I can't see you.

The man works a crack in the wall about half way down and sticks a hand through the space, wiggling his forefinger to get the woman to stoop down and see him.

Man: Hello. Look through here. You'll see my face.

Woman
[on knees,
all of this   Oh, I see you. I see your marigolds.
done slowly]: They need more sun.
Man: Let's shake on that.

First the man puts his hand through the wall and shakes on the woman's side of the wall, then she puts her hand through and shakes on his side of the wall. Then they part hands and look at each other's face.

Man: Now that you can see my face, don't you want
               to take the wall down?

The man and woman begin to take down the wall, huffing and puffing at the weight of the bricks. They move laboriously, two rows of bricks are still up as they begin to speak.

Man: It is hard work to take down this wall.
Woman: It has been up for so long, and it's jammed
               together with so much encrusted cement.
Man: You have to work very hard to take down a
               wall. Where do you get the strength to take
               down the wall?

The woman offers a personal reflection on how Christ, who "has broken down the dividing wall . . . between us" [Eph. 2:14b], empowers her to take down walls. The person playing this role can draw on her own personal experience or the life of the particular congregation where the sermon is being preached or both.

Woman: And where do you get the strength to take
               down the wall?

The man offers a personal reflection on how Christ, who "has broken down the dividing wall . . . between us" [Eph 2:14b], empowers him to take down walls. The person playing this role can draw on his own personal experience or the life of the particular congregation where the sermon is being preached or both.

They continue to take down the wall until it is fully dismantled.

Woman: Can you feel the wind blowing freely now that the wall is down?

Man: Yes, oh yes, I can. And can you see how the light shines on everything with fewer deep shadows?

Woman: I can. And it makes me so happy I want to rejoice and sing!

The entire congregation sings a hymn. One that celebrates the reconciling work of Christ would be particularly appropriate.

STRATEGY 4

Write the Sermon as a Movie Script

No matter who our favorite author is, many of us imagine our own cinematic version of the fiction we read. A movie runs in our head with every good scene. If a producer later makes a film from the same book, we will react on the basis of how closely the film matches our own imagining of the story.

This phenomenon suggests that another strategy for playing with images in the pulpit is to create the sermon as a film script or storyboard. Thinking about the angle of shots, fade-ins and fade-outs, what scenes will be spectacle, what scenes will be on a smaller scale—all of these can engage the congregation in the story by activating their own imaginations.

Something deeper may also happen. By using these cinemagraphic methods to explore the gospel, we suggest that people need not be captive to the slickly produced images of Hollywood. We invite them into stories that have the potential not only to entertain but to transform, and in doing this we come close to the spirit of Jesus' parables.

It is a mistake to overlook the popular appeal of the parables. Jesus was too great a preacher to make the bogus distinction between narrative and hard (rationalist) theology. He used wonderfully intriguing stories to draw people into a consideration of the deepest matters of God and grace. To a certain degree, Jesus' parables worked in his culture in the way movies do for us today: They provided a memorable narrative that could be passed on and retold again and again just as in the present day people will talk about their favorite scenes from a popular movie.

I hear many preachers who draw upon this technique in their sermons, often providing a theological perspective to a box office smash. Their preaching demonstrates to the congregation how the gospel provides a theological basis for responding to what the media present. Effective as this approach can be, I have something else in mind here: writing the sermon as though it were a movie script. Thus, in the sermon that follows I employ cinemagraphic writing to retell a parable about a great banquet, the kind of lavish scene that Hollywood loves to produce. By drawing upon that cinematic tradition while giving it the twist of grace that marks Jesus' parable, I hope to cast a critical doubt upon the values of extravagant wealth and power in our society.

An Unforgettable Dinner Party

Luke 14:15-24

Luke the evangelist
was among the avant-garde of early Christian communicators.
So if he were recounting this parable of Jesus today,
he might very well
make a movie of it.
I picture the story
done along the lines
of the recent movies,
Remains of the Day and *The Age of Innocence,*
both of which featured
lavish banquet scenes
taking place in cavernous rooms
at tables groaning
with rich food and wine

and set with dazzling crystal and silver
and decorated
with great candelabra.

In the original parable
on which the screen version would be based,
Luke indicates
the brash young preacher from Nazareth
was not talking about a potluck supper.
He calls it a "great banquet,"
and when people send their regrets
they do so with very proper and formal language:
"I pray you have me excused."

As Luke's cinematic epic begins
we see across the wide screen
in elegant gold letters,
the title:
An Unforgettable Dinner Party.
The credits fade
and the camera starts with a wide shot
of sumptuous formal gardens
with a huge and elegant mansion
in the background.
We hear the bright voices of a woman
and man talking on a veranda.
The camera pulls them into our vision.

They are in light summer clothing,
sitting in wicker chairs
sipping tea
and talking with their butler
as they plan a fabulous banquet.
There is something attractive about this couple
that goes deeper than their immediate appearance.
In their eyes

and the lines on their faces,
we see people who have known pain
and have gained wisdom.
And in their voices
we sense not a shred of arrogance,
but a gentleness that comes from the heart,
a graciousness that makes us feel as invited
as any guest on their list.

The butler is writing down
the invitation
as they want it to be engraved:
"We cordially request
the honor of your presence
at our banquet.
Limousine service will be provided."

From the way that the butler joins in the conversation,
it seems that he too owns the place,
and all three seem to share a single common character
of boundless grace and wisdom.

The scene fades,
and we see the entire household
staff preparing the mansion.
Windows are washed.
Floors are polished.
Long, heavy oak tables are set
with linen table cloth and napkins.
with china and crystal,
and so many knives and forks
you wonder which is for what.
Great bouquets of crimson roses
are placed on the tables.
And in the kitchen,
we see master chefs

roasting quail and pheasant.
Bakers prepare
triple chocolate cakes,
with quadruple chocolate icing.

This is to be
the most unforgettable dinner party
anyone has ever attended.

The great day arrives.
The woman comes down the stairs
in a sweeping, maroon velvet gown
with a diamond tiara
and the man is in formal attire.

Outside we see
a convoy of stretch limousines,
one after another
driving out through the gates of the great estate
to pick up all those who have been invited.

The camera focuses on one
particular limousine
that drives up to a major
corporate headquarters.
The chauffeur is shown into
the great central office
and announces to the C.E.O.
that the fabulous banquet is about to begin.
The C.E.O. says:
"I profoundly regret,
I cannot attend
the fabulous banquet
for I am just completing
a great merger with a Mexican firm
under the new terms of NAFTA."

Next we see
the same chauffeur
arriving at a fine home
and being greeted by
the owner who is coming out
the front door with a suitcase in hand,
who announces:
"I profoundly regret
I cannot attend
the fabulous banquet
for I have just bought a condominium
and am leaving for my first vacation there."

The chauffeur
drives down the street
to the next house on the list,
and finds a couple pulling out of the driveway.
"We profoundly regret
we cannot attend the fabulous banquet
for we have just been married
and are leaving on our honeymoon."

And now there follows
scene on scene,
one quick image
after another of
chauffeur after chauffeur
being turned down.

Eventually, we see all of the
limousines heading back to the mansion,
reforming the great convoy as they
pull in through the gates.

The chauffeurs
all run quickly
up the stairs into the banquet room.

It is a spectacular scene,
the first course has already
been placed on the table:
great silver platters
heaped with pâté, caviar,
cheeses, and fruit.
The champagne has been uncorked,
the candles have been lit.

When the host and hostess
find out no one has come,
they cry out with one voice:
"Go out quickly
to the streets and lanes of the city
and bring in the poor and maimed
and blind and lame."

Again we see the convoy
of great stretch limousines
go off through the gates.
Then the camera focuses on a single limo.

The chauffeur drives by a park
and sees two unshaven men
in frayed coats with moth-eaten sock hats.
The chauffeur slams on the brakes,
hops out, opens the door,
and says,
"Get in,
I'm taking you to the fabulous banquet."

One of them looks the chauffeur
in the eye and says,
"Yeah,
and my name is Donald Trump
and this is Marla."

But the chauffeur tugs them by the sleeve
into the car,
and shuts the door.

Next he stops at an alley way
where he sees a homeless woman
who has just tucked her two kids into bed
in a large carton.
"You and your kids
come and get in the car.
I'm taking you to a fabulous banquet."

She looks frightened
until one of the two men
in the back of the stretch limo
looks out the window
and says:
"Hi, Alice."
"What are you doing in there?" she says.
"We're going to a fabulous banquet.
Come join us."
So the woman gets her kids,
and they pile into the back of the limo,
and off they go.

Next the chauffeur stops
at some trash cans.
A man in a wheelchair
has the lids off
looking for some food.
This time the chauffeur only has to stop the car.
The two men in the back get out.
They recognize the man in the wheelchair
and in the twinkling of an eye,
they are helping their friend into the limousine

as they announce:
"We're going to a fabulous banquet."

Soon we see
chauffeur after chauffeur
inviting anyone they find
to get in their limousines
and come to the dinner party.

These individual shots fade
and we see the convoy of
limousines pulling up to the great entrance to the mansion.
Ramps have been put out
to make it accessible to wheelchairs.
Armies of people start arriving in the great hall.
At first they look around in wonder.
Alice's little girl
notes the diamond tiara on the hostess's head
and blurts out:
"Are those real diamonds?"
"Yes."
And with that the woman takes off the crown
and places it on the little girl's head.
One of the men in a torn sweatshirt
admires the host's dinner jacket,
and the host gives it to him to wear.

Although more people
keep coming and coming,
the hall never fills up.
There is always more room.

They begin to realize the food
really is theirs to eat.
At first they pick cautiously at their plates,
but soon they are enjoying everything with gusto.
And as they eat

and their glasses are filled,
they lose their awkwardness.
The hall begins to fill
with the murmur of people
telling stories and jokes,
laughing and crying together.

Music sounds and some get up to dance
and the dancing
and the feasting
and the joyful faces
are reflected off the diamonds
on the little girl's tiara
and we behold in dazzling light
the most unforgettable dinner party that ever was
and ever is to be.

STRATEGY 5
Use a Flashback

Here is a variation on writing the sermon as a movie script. It employs one of the most time-honored conventions in cinema, the flashback: The present moment fades away and we find ourselves witnessing what happened in the past. Everything we see is more poignant and intense because we view it from the perspective of the eventual consequences that flow from these earlier events.

Flashbacks were not invented with the camera. Storytellers, novelists, and dramatists have known for centuries the power of presenting a tale as someone's remembrance of the past. It is an effective method for three reasons. First of all, it helps us suspend our analytical judgments. The clouds of time and memory that surround the recall of any past event soften our critical vision.

Second, this method is in harmony with the way we search for meaning in our lives. We recall the stories of our past, reliving the feelings that they awakened at the time, seeing them in the changing light that comes with the progression of time, and distilling from all of this our identity, our sense of how the grief and joy of life have shaped us for better and for worse.

Finally, and perhaps most important for preachers, the flashback method helps to capture the way the memory of the community of faith worked both in Israel and in the church. When the Israelites celebrated the Exodus, they did not simply remember it as a past event, but its liberating power was released anew in the very act of their worship. Likewise, when the early church kept the Lord's Supper in "remembrance" of Christ, they had a sense of the risen Lord present among them. Worship is a flashback: a vivid replay of God's gracious acts that releases their holy power in the present moment. And when we preach using a flashback we reinforce this pattern of "traditioning" in the congregation, encouraging them to carry on the process of their remembering in light of how God has been at work in their lives so that they may serve God more faithfully in the present moment.

Flashbacks work well with biblical characters. When preachers are dealing with a text where a particular character appears (for example, Hebrews 11), it is revealing to look up other passages where the same figure appears. What were the events that shaped this human being, that brought the person to faith or doubt, to acts of love or injustice?

Because of the patriarchal bias of the culture out of which the scriptures arose, the Bible offers more material about men than women. However, new resources are helping us to recover more and more of women's stories in and behind the Bible so that the flashback has increasing possibilities for presenting women as well as men.[1]

The sermon that follows was specifically created to help a church celebrate its ministries of music. The fact that the focus was music immediately brought to mind the most famous musician in the Bible: David. Furthermore, music often touches off flashbacks in us. A song at our wedding, a hymn at a friend's funeral, a piece we played over and over during a time of crisis—any of these may for the rest of our lives awaken anew the original experience so that we relive it as vividly as if it were happening again. Tears or laughter, grief or joy return as clearly as the melody in our ears. Hence it seemed that a flashback method would be particularly effective in using David's ministry of music to illuminate the church's.

I do not worry whether or not the psalms ascribed to David were actually composed by him. The fact that he was credited with their composition even when he may not have composed them suggests that the guiding principle for understanding these matters is not literal accuracy, but spiritual vitality and theological depth. Thus, for example, the superscription to Psalm 51—"To the leader. A Psalm of David, when the prophet Nathan came to him, after he had gone in to Bathsheba"—reveals how seriously the community viewed such confession. It was no rote action. They understood that the necessity for it was rooted in radical evil.

The Wisdom of an Ancient Musician

2 Samuel 23:1-7

King David was unable to sleep.
He slowly got out of bed,
and walked across the room to the window.
Stars.
A sliver of pale moon.
David did not feel like a king anymore.
The years had worn him down.
Nowadays he hardly had energy enough
to lift his crown
and sit on his throne
and hold court.
David was tired of kingly duties.
He wanted to be done with them.

His old harp was on the table next to the window.
David couldn't remember when he last played the thing.
His hands were too stiff to move from string to string,
so he had given it up,
but he did not have the heart to dispose of the old instrument.
And now on this sleepless night,

attracted by the starlight
that glinted off the strings,
he walked over to the harp
and plucked a single note.
Pliiiing.
The sound faded on the air
but something stirred in David's heart.
It was the impulse to compose a song,
to write one last psalm to sing.
At the very thought of it,
the room seemed brighter,
his body more awake.
David wondered:
what should I write?
He plucked another string.
Pliiiiing.
And as its sound faded
his head filled with a melody from his youth.
He was a shepherd once again.
Out on the hills alone with the flock.
His chief entertainment
besides aiming stones at old clay jars with his sling
was making up songs,
picking out the tunes on his harp.
"The Lord is my shepherd I shall not want.
He makes me lie down in green pastures."
Maybe David's last song should be like that earlier one:
music for the lonely to invoke the presence of God.
That would be a great gift to leave behind.
Generations hence
when the community of faith celebrated the ministry of
music,
his song would help them remember
why music
is so important to the life of faith:
Music is prayer.

Music is the reach of the soul beyond itself.
Music is the assurance of the Spirit's eternal presence.

Pliiiing! Pliiing!
David plucked the harp again,
and found himself a young man
standing in the chambers of King Saul.
At first young David just stood before the great man.
Silent, awkward, not knowing what to do,
overwhelmed by the sudden change in his status:
in a matter of days
he had moved from shepherd
to an attendant in the king's court.
David was just a youth from the back hills.
He knew nothing about the ways of court and royalty.
Then he heard King Saul speaking.
It was a troubled voice,
not the resonance David expected from the leader of the
nation.
but plaintive and brooding:
"Play me something, Son.
Sing for me."
Young David picked up his harp.
He was nervous,
him, David, a shepherd from the countryside
playing for the king.
At first David's hands did not have their usual agility,
and his sweet voice was not as focused
as when he sang to himself and the sheep.
But the more David sang
the more King Saul settled back in his throne,
shutting his eyes,
the tense muscles in his face relaxing.
And when David saw this,
his playing took on its usual assurance,
and his voice floated sweetly on the air.

Would that be the theme of David's last song?—
the healing power of music.
That would be a great gift to leave behind.
Generations hence
when the community of faith celebrated the ministry of
music,
his song would help them remember
why music
is so important to the life of faith:
Music is a form of pastoral care.
Music is a way of restoring wholeness.
Music offers sanity to a world of mad power.

Pliiiing! Pliiing!
The memory of a popular song from the streets
marched through David's head:
"Saul has killed his thousands,
but David his tens of thousands."
It was an exaggeration.
But it was enough to make Saul wild with jealousy.
Saul turned against the young man
whose music he loved.
One day he hurled a spear at David
just missing him.
David had to flee for his life.
The terror and the sadness of those distant days
returned to David on this sleepless night.
As cruel as Saul had been to him,
David had never become bitter about the man.
Now standing at the window
and looking up at the stars,
David sang once again
the lament
that he had written
to commemorate the death of Saul
and Saul's son, Jonathan,

the dearest friend of David's life:
"How the mighty have fallen,
and the weapons of war perished!"
David found himself crying,
the tears burning with the memory
of one grief after another:
He remembered sending Uriah to his death
to cover up his adultery with Uriah's wife, Bathsheba.
Then the child she had born him died,
and David lamented in a psalm
"For I know my transgressions,
and my sin is ever before me . . .
Create in me a clean heart
and put a new and right spirit within me."
Would this be the theme
of David's last song before he died?—
That would be a great gift to leave behind.
Generations hence
when the community of faith celebrated the ministry of music,
David's song would help them remember
why music
is so important to the life of faith:
Music can be a prayer of confession,
Music can be a prayer of supplication.
Music can be the open heart surgery of the Spirit.

Pliiing.
Oh, if only that music of confession
had sounded in his son Absalom!
Absalom:
handsome,
gifted,
everyone's favorite.
But also: arrogant and rebellious.
When Absalom led the palace revolt against his own father,

David had done everything to save him,
personally instructing his own soldiers
the young man was not to be killed.
But Absalom was killed,
and David's music became the music of weeping,
the sound of inconsolable sorrow:
"O my son Absalom,
my son, my son Absalom!
Would I had died instead of you,
O Absalom, my son, my son!"
Would that be the theme of David's last song?—
music as the bearer of what words cannot bear.
That would be a great gift to leave behind.
Generations hence
when the community of faith celebrated the ministry of music,
David's song would help them remember
why music
is so important to the life of faith:
Music is the groaning of the Spirit,
Music is the prayer for which no speech is adequate.
Music is the aching and the yearning of the human heart.

The old king wiped the tears from his cheeks,
while all the melodies mixed together in his head at once:
the glad songs from his days as a shepherd,
the sweet lyrics that soothed Saul,
the laments of confession and grief,
the psalms of praise.
Then he reached out and plucked once again a single string:
Pliiiing!
The solitary tone upon the air
distilled from all the melodies in his head
one last song,
and he clearly saw
what he had sensed throughout his life:

the Spirit comes
through the ministries of music.
The Spirit comes through song
through
poetry,
melody,
rhythm,
harmony.
The Spirit visits us with a vision
of what is true and right and good.
The aged king opened his mouth to sing,
to sing the last song of his life.
He did not sing as a youth,
he was too old for that now.
He did not sing as a hero,
he was too aware of his own sins for that.
He did not sing as a warrior,
he was too frail for that now.
He did not sing to mourn others,
for he was about to join them.
He sang as an ancient musician
whose songs had led him to wisdom.
He sang as an instrument of the Spirit.
And this is what he sang:
"One who rules over people justly,
ruling in the fear of God,
is like the light of morning,
like the sun rising on a cloudless morning,
gleaming from the rain on the grassy land."
The old king stood at the window
singing his song,
its melody flowing out over the land.
And when he looked up,
every star in heaven
was singing with him.

STRATEGY 6

Reframe a Sacrament

Han van den Blink, a pastoral theologian and colleague, has a favorite verb that he often uses in helping individuals and organizations to understand their convoluted life situation: "reframe."[1] To reframe something is to look at it from a new perspective, to realize that our own viewpoint represents but one selected and organized version of the facts. I have watched Han van den Blink help people reframe situations that had them tied in knots. Suddenly, people began to talk with new insight that shone in their faces.

Good preaching often reframes a problem or a reality of Christian faith that has lost its original power for the congregation. For example, in recent decades most denominations have given increased attention to the sacrament of Baptism, providing new liturgical resources for its celebration through prayer and song. Among these resources has been the recovery of an ancient rite for the remembrance of our baptismal vows. This rite is not a second baptism. It is a way of recommitting ourselves to Jesus Christ and his ministry.

All of these resources—hymns, prayers, remembrance—are means of "reframing" the sacrament so that we sense anew the astounding grace of Jesus Christ in welcoming us into the church through baptism.

Preaching can join in this process of reframing, especially in an age when the media are redefining the symbols that communicate meaning within our cultures. The Christian sacraments are a powerful, visible sign or witness, which form us through imagery much more powerfully than the words that we attach for interpretation. We do not need to preach on the meaning of what we are doing every time we perform a sacrament. Such actions have their own way of evoking meaning through symbol and movement. But periodically it is helpful for preachers to reframe a sacrament or rite so that the congregation participates with fresh insight into its meaning and a keener sense of the Spirit's presence.

The sermon that follows is intended to precede either a baptism or a rite for the remembrance of baptism. It is essential that abundant water be poured out of a pitcher into a basin or font as part of the ritual that follows the sermon. A stingy little dribble will contradict the sermon!

Rising River

Ezekiel 47:1-6

Some mornings,
when I throw water in my face to wake up
and the water trickles down my forehead,
I find myself at age sixteen
standing in the upstairs room of the church
where I grew up.
I am being baptized.
I had not been baptized as an infant.
Jake Shaeffer,
the chief lay leader of the church,
is holding a large silver bowl of water,
and my pastor, Richard Weld,
is putting water on my head
and it is trickling down my forehead.
A trickle.
Just a few drops,
probably about the amount of water
that Ezekiel sees
in his fantastic vision

of a flow of water
that originates
as a few drops of water coming from the altar,
then gathering to a river
so great
one cannot pass through it.

When Ezekiel wrote this vision
the nation of Israel had been devastated.
Babylon had conquered and destroyed the city,
the foundations of belief and culture
lay in ruin.
A heavenly figure,
an angel,
comes and shows the prophet this vision
of a trickle of water flowing out of the altar.
Just a droplet.
A droplet about as large as the drop of water
coming down my head when I was age sixteen.
There I was
being asked the central question of life:
"Do you believe in Jesus Christ
and will you trust him
and love and serve him
all the days of your life?"
There I was,
too embarrassed to ask Janet,
my girlfriend back then,
to dance with me when certain boys were present.
There I was avoiding peanut butter and chocolate,
and there I was being asked
this profound question of existence
and saying, "Yes."
How much knowledge and faith did I have?
Just a trickle.
Just a droplet.

And the heavenly figure
led the prophet Ezekiel out a thousand cubits,
and behold the stream that started as a trickle
was ankle deep.
I remember a time in my life
when I became aware that the stream was growing deeper,
the stream of faith,
the stream of grace and assurance.
I was a college student.
Through the chaplain's office
I had become the Youth Director
in an inner-city African American Church.
I had been raised in an Anglo church
in upstate New York,
and I can recall
when I was placed in that inner-city church.
It was the sixties.
I wondered what would my reception be.
How would I manage to relate to a culture
and a people that were very different from me?
The young people,
ranging from grade school
into high school,
were gracious toward me.
They were glad that I had come to their inner-city church.
It was in a distressed neighborhood.
We used to go out and do activities in the backyard
and we constantly had to keep our eyes
on the ground
because there was so much broken glass and debris.
Much as we had cleaned up
somebody could easily be cut and injured.
One evening,
as the sun was setting
and we were finishing our session together
—I don't know what moved me other than the Spirit—

I said,
"Let's just hold our hands in a circle
and say the Lord's Prayer."
This took place
during a time of brutal confrontation in the United States
between blacks and whites,
segregationists and integrationists.
I remember praying,
"Our Father who art in heaven, Thy kingdom come"
and I looked down
and at my feet
I saw broken glass.
Then I looked up and out
and saw some winos on the street.
"Thy will be done
on earth as it is in heaven."
I looked around at all those young black faces
knowing what hatred they faced.
When we finished and said "amen,"
several of them were crying
and two came up and embraced me
and behold
the stream of grace
had come up to my ankles.

And the angel of the Lord
led the prophet Ezekiel out a thousand cubits farther
and behold the stream that had started as a trickle at the altar
had become knee deep.
I remember a time when the stream was knee deep.
I had been through a terrible tragedy.
The details are not necessary for me to relate
because all of you
have your own deep tragedies.
At the time I wondered
how in the world would I ever get through this.

But one who was a great friend
got me through.
And behold,
the river of grace and love had come up to my knees.
Then I became a pastor
and I delighted
in the joys and privileges of being a pastor.
I cannot imagine any calling in the world
more profoundly satisfying.
To be with people at the times
of their greatest need
and their gladdest celebrations,
to preach Jesus Christ,
to bring healing in his name.
But again and again:
the phone ringing in the night,
rivalries springing up in the church,
horrendous conflicts in the surrounding community.
And yet
now and then
someone would come
as a messenger of grace.
I think of a man named Howard.
He and I disagreed on everything
except God,
the wonder of God,
the grace of God,
the love of God.
This we held in common.
One day I was visiting him
and I said a prayer with him
and he said to me,
"You know, Tom,
I loved your praying for me.
I think I ought to pray for you."
Howard prayed:

"O God,
Tom needs a lot of help.
He doesn't see anything the way I do.
He really needs help,
but he is a good pastor
and I want him to be assured of your love for him."
Behold,
the river had come up to my waist.

And the Angel of the Lord
took the prophet Ezekiel
a thousand cubits more
and the river had become such a vast torrent
that none could pass over it.
From a trickle of love,
from a trickle of faith and justice,
from a trickle of compassion,
a river so great that none could pass over it,
and on its shores grew trees of life
that produced fruit for nurture
and leaves for healing.

I wish I could say to you,
I have seen the river that deep,
but I have not
and yet I know it is only such a river
filled with that much love and justice
that can redeem and heal this world.
Although I have not yet seen it,
I trust the angel that came to Ezekiel:
I believe the river is that deep.
So if all we feel in our life
is a trickle of grace,
the merest drop of faith,
then let us remember
the vision the angel gives to Ezekiel:

a trickle of love and grace
can become a river of a society transformed
and personal lives remade,
a river of peace for the whole world.
This is a vision that can come true in our lives.
The place to start
is to take a sip
from the one who says to us,
"Whoever drinks of the water that I give
will never thirst.
The water that I shall give
will become in them a spring of water
welling up to eternal life."

As a transition to the baptism or rite of baptismal remembrance, sing "Shall We Gather at the River" or some other hymn with language invoking the living streams of God.

STRATEGY 7
Let a Little Child Lead You

Children have a lot to teach us, or more accurately, to re-teach us: things we have forgotten as we have taken on the increasing burdens of adult sophistication and responsibility. Youngsters help us recall the elemental simplicities of our lives, our basic fears and dreams, our unfiltered responses to the beauty and terror of life: how sun throws diamonds on the water, the way clouds form monsters in the sky and trees whisper to us in the wind and a bedroom fills with ghosts when the light is turned off.

These elemental simplicities open us to wonder, to faith, to the recognition of how tiny and frail we are before the vastness of creation. We sometimes need to let a little child lead us, to take us to treasures that we buried and forgot as we grew up. A child can lead us not only in a children's sermon but in an adult sermon when the preacher recounts the actions of a child. If the story is not too cute, if it involves some primary life experience, it will often result in a sermon that works at multiple levels of knowledge.

The various new media (film and multimedia) have discovered what centuries of poets, writers, and family raconteurs have known: that nostalgia, as experienced through narrative in our family history, is a deep-seated yearning. The child leans forward to hear a parent's memory:

> I remember, I remember,
> The house where I was born,

> The little window where the sun
> Came peeping in at morn . . .[1]

The same need can be tapped as children and adults listen to the sermon together, each of them "getting the sermon" through their own way of perceiving and knowing.

In the sermon that follows, two children lead us: One is afraid of the dark, another afraid of the water. I have generally found such stories to be among the most effective in the pulpit. They are simultaneously resonant with primal human experience and the primal imagery of the Bible.

Children may not understand the connections that the sermon draws between the stories and the passage from Hebrews, but even then they will be learning something very important: The Bible is about my life, my fears and joys. And they will sense how precious they are in the eyes of God, for a child's story is worthy of an adult sermon.

You Go First

Hebrews 12:1-2

When I was in college,
I used to baby-sit
for a six-year-old boy named Peter.
His mother started hiring me
after her husband had died.
I recall putting Peter to bed.
The house was very old.
Over the years
various owners had added on to it
section by section.
The electrical system
must have been an afterthought.
There was only one way to switch on the light
at the end of the upstairs hall

where Peter's bedroom was located:
You had to turn at a right angle to the staircase
and grope along the hall to his door
until you felt the switch with your hand.
Whenever we were downstairs watching television
and it was time for bed,
Peter would stare into the darkness
at the top of the stairs
and say to me:
"You go first."
I would start upstairs alone,
and just as I was getting to the top step
I would hear footsteps behind me.
Then Peter's hand
was in mine,
and I groped along the wall
and found the switch.

What struck me about this
is that Peter did not wait for me to turn on the light.
It was enough
simply to know I was there in the dark.
"You go first,"
he had said,
and as long as I did go first,
then he had the courage
to follow after me.

I remember Peter's hand in mine to this day,
not just because it charmed me,
but because it touched
something profound
that I have observed is true in myself
and others:
the great hunger of the human heart
to trust

that there is some power,
some strength,
some hand
waiting to take
ours in the shadows of the unknown.

The writer of Hebrews
knew about this hunger.
The letter is addressed to Christians
who are facing a frightening
and uncertain future.
It is sometime around the year
A.D. 100
so these people
represent the third and fourth generations of Christians.
They can recall the faith
of their grandparents
who had eagerly expected
the return of Jesus.
And, as the writer of Hebrews
reminds them,
there was a time
when their own faith was strong.
And they had stood up
to threats and public torment.
But now
that strong, clear faith
was slipping away.
Christ had not returned.
Persecution was increasing.
The future looked grim.
The initial enthusiasm of faith
was waning
and the community was unraveling.

What in the world
would give those Christians the courage

to move boldly into the future?

The writer of Hebrews
tells them:
Christ has gone first.
Christ is already leading the way.
"Let us run with perseverance
the race that is set before us,
looking to Jesus the pioneer and perfecter of our faith,
who for the sake of the joy that was set before him
endured the cross."
Christ has gone first.
Christ is in front of us
beckoning us on.

Peter, the little boy in my charge,
said,
"You go first."
That was thirty years ago,
but recently I saw the story replayed
while sitting on the edge of a swimming pool.
I watched a mother already in the water
and her little girl
in a life jacket
on the deck of the pool
trying to jump in.
The child would approach the pool
very slowly.
Tiny steps.
She got right to the edge.
And she started squatting down
as if to spring up over the water.
But instead,
she stood back up
and grimaced.
Her whole body

said,
"Do I want to do this or not?"
Again and again
she would get poised to jump,
then stand up
and stare suspiciously at the water.
But all the while
her mother was in the pool
right in front of her.
Her mother started reaching out her arms.
She was saying:
"Come on, Honey.
I'm right here.
You'll be fine."
And finally
the little girl sprang up into the air
and came down into the pool
with a splash.
Her mother caught her
and the two of them laughed with delight.

Many of us
relive the pattern of that little girl
when we face what is
unfamiliar and fearful:
a new stage of life,
a new location,
a world that no longer runs
like the world we grew up in,
an unforeseen challenge to live our faith,
to carry on the ministry of Christ
in places and ways that unnerve us.

Christ has gone first.
Christ is like that mother.
Christ is standing

ready to catch us
and calling to us:
"Come on, dear ones.
Plunge in.
I've gone first.
I'm right here.
You'll be fine."

As if it were not enough
that Christ has gone first,
the writer of Hebrews
reminds us of generation after generation
of faithful heroes and heroines
in the Hebrew Scripture
who preceded Christ.
Chapter 11,
is the prelude to the verses we have read.
It is a litany of women and men
who "by faith" endured
every form of suffering and pain and disillusionment.
The author gathers them all together
in a dramatic image
calling them a cloud of witnesses.
This cloud surrounds us,
ready to cheer us on
as if we were about to begin a long-distance race
in a vast athletic stadium.
We can hear them cheering,
the roar of their encouragement.
The writer of Hebrews is there,
calling out
"lay aside every weight and sin
that clings so closely to us."

For a moment,
our hearts grow faint.

We think we don't have what it takes,
but then the crowd begins
a great chant:
"Run the race,
run the race!
Look to Jesus,
look to Jesus!"

As we run,
their cheers sometimes
seem to fade to silence,
but now and then we come around
a corner in the course
and we catch their voices once again.
"Run the race,
run the race!
Look to Jesus,
look to Jesus!"

I can think of times
when I have heard them,
loud and distinct.
There was a time of great sadness
when my wife held me
and I heard them through her presence:
"Run the race,
run the race!
Look to Jesus,
look to Jesus!"

There was a time
when I was teaching,
in an ecumenical group of African American churches,
more than thirty-five students
including some twenty or more women.
They had been through the wars

of discrimination and bigotry,
women who stand against all that is working to destroy
their children and their neighborhoods.
When those women would rise in class to pray,
to preach,
to sing,
I could hear the whole cloud of heaven's witnesses
singing:
"Run the race,
run the race!
Look to Jesus,
look to Jesus!"

And there have been countless times in church
when I have come forward to the altar
bearing with me
the burdens that are common
to the humanity of us all,
and as I was receiving the sacrament
and listening to the choir
I heard a deeper music
in the music they were singing,
and it was the music of the cloud of witnesses:
"Run the race,
run the race!
Look to Jesus,
look to Jesus!"

Those are among the times
when I have heard the great cloud of witnesses.
When have you heard the cloud?
Think now:
When have you heard those witnesses,
calling to you
"Run the race,
run the race!

Look to Jesus,
look to Jesus!"
Perhaps you heard them
and did not realize it.
Perhaps it was
a surge of hope in your heart
when things looked hopeless.
Perhaps it was a friend's encouragement.
Perhaps it was a moment
of silent prayer so still
that it was filled with
a mysterious sense of presence.
Perhaps it was a time
when you stood against an injustice
and your knees were shaking
and your voice quivering
but you heard inside
a voice crying out for what is
right and good and just.

Or perhaps
you have been running
for a stretch without
the sound of the cloud of witnesses
in your heart.
Then listen this week
with renewed attentiveness
for their voices of encouragement.
For when you hear them,
you will see
that Christ has gone first
and you will receive
the grace and strength
to follow him.

STRATEGY 8
Play a Game

"Mere child's play" is not so "mere" as a workaholic society might think. Play is essential to a child who is trying out roles, rules, and possibilities, and play does not end with childhood. Adult play can extend from the playing of brain teaser games on the computer to playing instruments, to the playfulness of mind that allows us to entertain dreams and visions that our daily routines suppress and ignore. Play

> provides spaces in which the modern human is in search of meaning or, to adopt a Jungian phrase, "in search of a soul." Religion, theater, therapy, or other hybrid spaces are perhaps the few remaining forums within an increasingly technological and pragmatic society in which meaning can be created, reinvented, rearranged, probed, and played with. In playing, we become human.[1]

Unfortunately, there has often been a bias against play, sometimes reinforced by a grim religiosity. For example, here is an instruction published by an American church in 1792: "We prohibit play in the strongest terms. . . . The students shall be indulged with nothing which the world calls play."[2] It is predictable that the personal computer, which now rivals the automobile as a necessity for human commerce and communication, is primarily used for playing games in the home. Many of these games, designed especially for adolescent males, are horrific and violent. As a critical and powerful alternative, the renewing power of religious realities requires that we be able to play them out in our worship and daily lives:

> Transformed reality, as we encounter it in art and religion, remains meaningless unless humans appropriate them through play. Music needs to be performed, drama staged, and religious rites enacted to be understood. Without play, they have no meaning.[3]

"The Shepherds' Game,"[4] which is described below, allows an entire congregation to join in the Christmas story. It is an intergenerational event, and indeed gains in playfulness and richness of meaning when every generation is involved.

I have played this game with many different congregations and groups over the years, and have then drawn on the experience of the game to supply the insights of the sermon.

The Shepherds' Game

Luke 2:8-14

Goal of the Game:

To search as shepherds for the infant Jesus and in doing so to discover what is involved in trusting the Good News of his birth.

Preparations Ahead of Time:

1. Set up certain rooms in the church as "households" and put a poster on each household identifying it as "household 1," "household 2," and so forth. You will need one household for every two to three groups of shepherds. Each group should consist of five to seven persons. In each household

there will be a person whose purpose is to discourage the shepherds' search as a wild goose chase. But if the householder fails to do this, then she or he must tell the shepherds to open envelope five. (Envelopes are described below.)

2. Set up other rooms as inns, at least three of them: "Red Lion Inn," "Bear Inn," and so on. These rooms should be as far away as possible from the place where the congregation initially gathers at the start of the game. It is important that people come to the rooms marked "household" before they know there are rooms marked as inns.

In each inn, except for one, the innkeeper will claim to know where the Messiah is and will invite the people in. Once they are in the room the innkeeper is to present a messianic political program, or Christ in art, or some fad or scheme that promises salvation.

Only one innkeeper will know where the child is. If the shepherds ask, "Where is the Messiah?" this innkeeper responds, "What are you talking about?" because this innkeeper has no idea that it is the Messiah who has been turned away from the inn. The shepherds will have to discover to ask if the innkeeper knows where an infant is, to which the innkeeper will reply, "O, yes, in the manger" and then give them directions.

3. Set up a beautiful manger scene in a far-off room or in the cellar. Someone will be there to tell the shepherds they have found the Christ, that they may offer prayer and then open envelope number six, which instructs them to return to their flocks, the room where it all started.

4. Have someone dress as a Roman centurion with a spear and shield. He has the authority to threaten people with arrest and with death if he catches them wandering the streets a second time. He has a jail where he can throw them. They can escape if it is not guarded. They can try to convert him to join the search. He can decide whether or not to join them. None of this is announced ahead of time. It is a surprise element in the game.

5. Prepare sets of the following six envelopes. You will need one full set for each group of five to seven shepherds.

Envelope #1: You have heard the angels say the Messiah is born. Do you believe this or is it madness? If you decide it is not worth your attention, open no more envelopes and stay here until the game is over. If you decide to trust the chorus of angels, open envelope #2.

Envelope #2: You have decided to go search for the Messiah. What will you take for a gift? Once you have decided this as a group, open envelope #3.

Envelope #3: Now decide what you will do with your sheep. You cannot drive them all there. Once you have decided, open #4.

Envelope #4: Go to household _____ to ask directions. Search for the household in the education wing.[5] If another group is in the household, wait patiently until they come out. No matter what that group says when they are leaving the house, you must go in and hear what the householder has to say.

Envelope #5: Go searching for inns and ask if the innkeeper knows where the Messiah is.

Envelope #6: Return to your flocks where you heard the angel's announcement and the heavenly host and discuss what you learned about searching for the Christ.

Playing the Game

1. Meet in the main worship area of your church or your church hall, explaining that you are the game director. If questions arise players can come to you.

2. Break people into groups of five to seven, and tell them they are all shepherds.

3. Give each group one set of the six messages, each message sealed in its own envelope with the number marked on the outside. It is usually best to give the set to an adult with whom you have reviewed the general concept of the game ahead of time, but without giving away any of the details.

4. Explain to all the groups that the goal is to find the infant Jesus, but the goal is not to rush to get there. There is no prize for being first. Instead, the goal is to work their way as a group through the six envelopes. They may not go on to the next envelope until they have completed the task given in the preceding envelope.

5. Read the announcement of Christ's birth to the shepherds, Luke 2:8-14. You must stop at verse 14 because the participants are the shepherds and the rest of the game involves their completing the story by how they play the game.

6. Have the choir or soloist sing an appropriate hymn or anthem after the reading of the scripture. Do not use canned Christmas music of the kind that you might hear at the shopping mall. It awakens too much of the commercial spirit and puts the game in the wrong perspective.

7. Tell people they may begin.

Reflecting upon the Experience

As groups return they can talk among themselves, reviewing what happened to them and what they learned about searching for Christ. When all are back, you as game director will go through the six envelopes in order, asking each group to tell in a few sentences how they handled the challenge of that envelope, what their most crucial experience was.

Keep this moving.

Do not let anyone go on too long.

Have somebody taping or writing down the responses because these are going to provide the substance of the sermon.

At the end of this reflection session, announce you will be drawing all of this together in a sermon to be preached on

_____.

Then, after the entire group sings a joyful carol, serve refreshments. Be prepared for a lot of people to come and tell you their experiences and insights on an individual basis. Every time I have offered the game I have been swamped with such reflections.

Preparing the Sermon

Let the order of the envelopes give you the outline of the sermon. Then review the responses. You cannot use everything! But you will be able to draw upon a considerable amount.

Here is a sermon based on actual experiences and responses to the game.

Far More Than a Plaster-of-Paris Jesus

Last week we played "the shepherds' game."
We gathered here
and pretended we were the shepherds
hearing the announcement of Christ's birth.
We were in groups of five to seven,
from children
to the oldest.
Each group had six envelopes,
which it had to open one at a time.
The first envelope said:

You have heard the angels say the Messiah is born. Do you believe this or is it madness? If you decide it is not worth your attention, open no more envelopes and stay here until the game is over. If you decide to trust the chorus of angels, open envelope #2.

One of you played the skeptic
and said,
"I'm not sure if I do believe it."
And you dropped out,
and were satisfied to sit here
until the others returned
filled with interesting stories.
Then you said,
"I wish I had gone."
I wonder how many of us
at the end of this season,
will say,
"I wish I had gone.
Gone to Bethlehem.
Gone to see the Christ,
but something held me back,
some internal voice
I wish I had not listened to."

The second envelope said:

You have decided to go search for the Messiah. What will you take for a gift? Once you have decided this as a group, open envelope #3.

It was such fun
to see some of you emptying out
pocketbooks and wallets,
searching for something to give Christ.
Some of you considered giving him
tissues,
a pocketknife,

a safety pin,
some pocket change,
and then a lot of you said
you would take some sheep,
and several decided you would offer
your hearts, your minds, your lives to Christ.
Is Christ on your gift list this year?
What will you give him?

The third envelope said:

Now decide what you will do with your sheep. You cannot
drive them all there. Once you have decided, open #4.

Some groups were so caught up in the moment
that they decided
just to leave their sheep
and go for broke.
Some individuals volunteered to stay
while the rest of their group left on the search.
Some drew lots to decide who would be left behind.
One group kept sending back reports
to the shepherd they had left behind,
and when they found Christ,
they came back,
and while some of them
now took care of the sheep
the others led him to Christ.
Upon hearing of this,
some groups regretted
they had not thought to do the same,
because they wanted everyone included.
How will we include everyone
in the Good News of Christ?
It is not always easy to know how.
But that one group came up with a way.

Maybe there are strategies
that we as a church,
we as a pack of shepherds,
have never considered.

The fourth envelope said:

Go to household _____ to ask directions. Search for
the household in the education wing. If another group is
in the household, wait patiently until they come out. No
matter what that group says when they are leaving the
house, you must go in and hear what the householder has
to say.

This is where the search got nasty.
People ran into hard-nosed skeptics.
Householders angry to be awakened from their sleep.
Folks who said
the search for the Messiah
is nothing but a wild goose chase.
Folks who tried
to talk the shepherds into
returning to their flocks.
They said,
"You are following a fool's dream."
And some of you later confessed
you got discouraged.
But in every case,
most people in the group
refused to give up
so that even those who were discouraged
stayed with the search for Christ.
That is why we need one another:
Every one of us
has our times of bright faith
and our times of doubt

and we need one another
to pull each other through the times of doubt.

But then as you left the houses,
many of you ran into the Roman centurion.
You discovered
that this religious journey
is not safe and easy.
Several of you tried to convert the centurion!
And he shared later
that he was bound and determined
not to be converted
because he wanted to keep the game realistic
with the brutality of the world.
But when one of the children
took his hand
and said,
"Come on you gotta see this,"
the centurion's heart melted
and he threw down his spear.
Sentimental and unrealistic?—
that may be what our minds tell us,
but somewhere in our hearts
we know there is great truth in what happened:
It sometimes takes
a little child
to lead us
to the child whose birth we celebrate.

The fifth envelope said:

Go searching for inns and ask if the innkeeper knows where
the Messiah is.

One innkeeper had pictures of great Christian art
and coffee, milk, and Christmas cookies.

She had set up the inn so beautifully
that you thought you really
had found the Christ.
And then were you disappointed
when you learned
that you had stopped the search prematurely.
Although later on,
one of you said:
"But Christ was there.
In the beauty.
In the hospitality and fellowship."
That was not the way we planned the game,
but of course, that is the way it is:
We don't control where Christ is.
And it sounds as though
the group that stayed and enjoyed
the beauty of the art
and the hospitality of that innkeeper
did in truth find Christ
in a different way
than we game organizers had planned.
Who knows how and where
Christ is going to surprise any of us,
coming in ways beyond
all our calculations and imaginings.

The sixth envelope said:

Return to your flocks where you heard the angel's announcement and the heavenly host and discuss what you
learned about searching for the Christ.

There were so many learnings
and yet the one
that seemed to strike so many of us with great power
was the one near the end:

"I loved playing this game,
but as I walked away from the creche set
in the cellar
back to the sanctuary
I realized
I want far more
than a plaster-of-Paris Jesus.
I want what we sing:
'Be born in us today.'
Then it won't be just a game.
It will be our whole life."

STRATEGY 9

Listen to the Muffled Voices

Some mornings when I am watching the news on television, I channel surf among the major networks to see if they are reporting the same or different matters. There is a striking similarity, not only in what are chosen as the top stories, but also in the way they are presented: the same sound bite, the same scene repeated again and again. For all that we hear about choice and diversity of content, it is amazing how much imitation we see. We always hear from a few prominent voices, those with power and the ability to grab the attention of media by virtue of their position or their glamour as televisual subjects. Those who struggle day by day to survive are not the newsmakers.

But before preachers become haughty about the media, we need to examine how we use the Bible. It is easy for sermons to become like the media's cameras, always focusing on the same characters, and not giving adequate play to those voices that have been buried by our constant attention to the chief players. One of the most significant gifts to preaching from liberation and feminist theologies has been the way they have helped us recover the muffled voices that are in the Bible and in our world. This act of recovery often breaks open texts so that the light of God streams from the familiar story with dazzling brightness.[1]

I cannot change who I am or the past that I bring to the act of preaching. But I can by reading and listening and imagining come to have at least some idea of the world of other people, especially those whose voices have been muffled. Indeed, the ability to imagine another's world is the prerequisite for all acts of communication and compassion. Adrian M. S. Piper describes this under the term "modal imagination," and acknowledges that entering another's world can be transformative of our own conventional imagination:

> I read a first-person account by a battered wife of her experiences, and my emotions as well as my thoughts are fully engaged, not only as I am reading but afterward as well. My imaginative reconstruction replaces reality as I am absorbing her story and alters my view of the world afterward.[2]

Notice that it is emotion as well as thought that is engaged in altering our view of the world. Although entertaining new ideas is part of the process, genuine transformation always reaches into the depths of feeling.

The next sermon starts with an experience of my own that gives me at least a glimpse into the much greater terror that the sermon addresses. The use of my experience is intended to invite those who currently possess power and status to think of those times when they did not enjoy these privileges, when they felt their vulnerability as human beings. Instead of fleeing from the memory of those experiences, we need to let them awaken our capacities to extend justice and compassion to those who suffer without protection in this cruel world.

Dropping Our Weapons

John 8:2-11

It was a Saturday night in late spring.
I had walked the mile from my house to church
to get a book from my study
for the sermon in the morning.
On the way home

three drunk teenagers jumped me
and started pounding and kicking me.
In the head,
in the chest,
below the belt.
I saw car lights coming
down the other side of the road,
and I waved and screamed,
but the car was moving fast
and I am not sure
the driver even saw us.
Then I noticed another car with high beams
coming down our side of the road.
I yelled "Look!"
quickly, at the top of my lungs,
almost barking like a dog.
I must have startled my assailants
because they looked up
straight into the headlights.
Blinded by the brightness
they released their grasp,
and I ran as fast as I have ever run in my life.
When I got home,
afraid they might jump
the next person to come down the lane,
I called the police.
The person at the switchboard asked:
"Did this happen in the village
or beyond the village sign?"
"What does it matter?"
"We have to establish jurisdiction."
"Look, I have just been mugged.
It's a warm night.
Somebody else could go for a walk
and get roughed up
if not worse."

I do not recall the rest of the conversation
except that no one was sent even to investigate.
When I hung up,
the adrenaline left my body
and my knees gave way
and I found myself shaking all over.

Not for one moment
would I compare what I went through
to the victims of chronic violence and abuse.
Nevertheless,
I have often reflected on that brutal moment
to gain at least a glimmer
of what it is like to face abuse
again and again
and not to have the resources
or support
to escape.

It is even worse
when religious and social systems
reinforce and justify the violence.
The woman taken in adultery
faces the full force of such terror.
Her accusers bring her before Jesus.
"Now in the law
Moses commanded us to stone such women.
Now what do you say?"
Why do they challenge Jesus
on this particular point of law,
why make this a test case?
Is it because of his openness to women?
Do they fear
Jesus is weakening
their male prerogatives?
Whatever the reason,

Jesus does not give them an instant response.
He writes in the sand with his finger.
This was the ancient custom
of one called to render judgment.
Jesus takes his time at it
while they keep questioning him,
as if to rush the court judgment.

What is Jesus writing?
Does he write down the law
which they have only partially cited?—
"If a man commits adultery with the wife of his neighbor,
both the adulterer and adulteress
shall be put to death."
Both the man and the woman
are to be stoned.
The men claim
they took the woman
"in the very act of adultery."
But they have brought only the woman.
Does Jesus write in the sand:
"Where
is
the
man?"
While they keep questioning him
and he keeps writing
does he think back to other stories
in the tradition
involving the terrible abuse and violence
done to women?
Jesus knows the tradition
so it is not wild to speculate
that he may be recalling
what Phyllis Trible
has titled "texts of terror."

Perhaps Jesus remembers Judges 19, which recounts
the betrayal,
rape,
torture,
and dismemberment
of an unnamed woman.

How can a religious community
break the grip of abuse?
Surely one part of it
is never to forget the past:
the utter horror of what has been done.
At the end of Judges 19, the writer commands:
"Consider it,
take counsel,
and speak out."

Perhaps all
or some
or none of these things
fill Jesus' considerations
as he writes with his finger in the sand.
But then he looks up
and we know what he says:
"Let anyone among you
who is without sin
be the first
to throw a stone at her."
Jesus breaks the men's projections,
their propensity to make the woman
bear the weight of their own wrongs and anxieties.
Jesus bends down to write again.
The men leave.
One by one.
They came as a mob.
They leave as individuals,

each compelled
to come to terms with his own sin.
Those carrying rocks in their hands
drop them.
Thud.
Thud.
Thud.
They drop their weapons.
And not only the rocks.
Their other weapons as well:
arrogance,
male privilege,
self-righteousness.
What is Jesus writing as they leave?
Is he writing
some of the common sexist maxims of his age?
"At the birth of a boy all are joyful,
but at the birth of a girl all are sad."
"Even the most virtuous of women is a witch."
Let us not be arrogant ourselves
and think these are ancient sentiments long dead.
Listen to locker-room talk.
Read what is written in public restrooms.

Perhaps the second time Jesus writes in the sand
he writes
something to counter the debasement of women,
something that represents the riches and wisdom
of the Hebraic tradition.
Perhaps he is writing:
"God created humankind in his image,
male and female he created them."
Perhaps Jesus looks at that great verse from Genesis,
and then crosses out
the maxims that would deny its truth.
Now the only words that remain

are the biblical affirmation
that women and men
bear equally the image of God.

Jesus looks up
and tells the woman he does not condemn her.
And then he says
"Go, and sin no more."
The most common interpretation
of that final instruction is:
"Go, and do not commit adultery again."
But perhaps that is not all there is to it.
Perhaps the sin
that the woman most needs to avoid
is forgetting her infinite value
in the eyes of God.
Perhaps Jesus is telling her
always to remember
that she bears the image of her creator,
and that image grants her
a dignity,
value,
and
strength
that no man can ever take away.

We do not know what happens to this woman afterward.
I would like to think
she goes on to claim
the new life Christ has offered her.
But John does not tell us.
What we know is this:
The brutality goes on in our own society.
And the bruised bodies
and the blood of our sisters

are still
crying, crying from the ground.
"Consider it,
take counsel,
and speak out."

STRATEGY 10
Compare Translations

The strategies in this book have been aimed at ways of making our sermons more visual and dramatic in order to engage a culture whose receptive capacities have been conditioned by the mass media and the recently converging media. Although the process of creating these sermons involved exegetical work with the biblical texts, the content of the sermons has not focused on the details of a close reading. My goal has been, instead, to convey the spirit of the scripture for our own time. However, a variety of strategies is essential to maintaining the vitality of the congregation's receptivity, and one effective strategy is to examine the textual details in the body of the sermon itself.

The next sermon is based on John 9:1-11, the giving of sight to a man blind since birth. I came to the passage for a healing service. Though sponsored by a particular church, the service was ecumenical in its outreach and had become an annual tradition. In its early years the service was specifically an attempt to support the victims of AIDS and those ministering to them. But more recently, without weakening its original intention, the service has expanded to include all who desire a service of healing.

A service of healing is an effective strategy for presenting the gospel because it engages the senses of the human body completely. People coming forward for anointing and prayer is such a powerful symbolic action, that the sermon does not need to compete with the drama of the ritual. The sermon can afford to focus more on the complexities of language. The contrast in the means of communication will strengthen the effectiveness of both sermon and rite.

A section of John's story about the blind man has always been theologically problematic for my understanding of God's compassion, and the New Revised Standard Version does not reduce the problem. Here is Jesus' response to the question of whether the man was born blind because he or his parents sinned:

> Neither this man nor his parents sinned; he was born blind so that God's works might be revealed in him.

Although the opening phrase is helpful in reducing the blame and guilt that people often feel about illness, the second phrase—especially the conjunction "so that"— sounds as if God deliberately had the man born blind in order to manifest his power. Such theology might reinforce the cruelty that many sick people, especially AIDS patients, have faced: namely, being told that God willed their illness for some purpose, be it for punishment or some mysterious reason beyond mortal comprehension. The church ought not to add this heavy theology onto people already burdened by illness and all its attendant fears.

So I began to compare translations and discovered that the following is an equally valid rendering of the Greek text:

> His blindness has nothing to do with his sins or his parents' sins. But that God's power might be seen at work in him, we must keep on doing the works of him who sent me as long as it is day.[1]

In this translation Jesus shifts our focus away from trying to establish ultimate causes of illness and disability. Instead of expending energies on a theological puzzle no one has ever solved, we are to give ourselves to the act of healing.

Comparing translations becomes in this sermon a strategy for removing the burden of a theology that might crush the spirits of the afflicted rather than lift them up.

No Name, No Face

John 9:1-11

How many times
had the neighbors
seen the man?
When they left for work
in the morning,
there he was,
on the corner
at his usual post:
the blind man,
his hand stretched out
for some loose change.
And when they came home,
he was usually still there.
And when they went off
on errands,
they saw him again.

"The blind man"—
that's how the neighbors referred to him.
According to the gospel,
they never called him by name.
He was to them:
"the blind man."
They had seen him
begging year after year
until you would think
his face
was etched on their memory.

But when Jesus restores
the man's sight,
a debate breaks out
among the neighbors.
Some say:
"That's the man
who was born blind."
But others dispute it:
"No, it just looks like him."
They saw the man
for years.
So why can't they recognize him now?
I suppose many of them
had never looked at his face.
They had never
studied his features,
but had simply walked by him
day after day,
year after year,
thinking,
"Oh, there's the blind man."

To them he had
no name,
no face.

In their minds
his blindness
completely defined who he was.
They never thought
of him as someone
who, like themselves,
hoped and dreamed,
laughed and wept,
someone who relished
the smell of roasting nuts

and the taste of cheese,
someone who loved
the warmth and touch
of another body beside him.
Someone who was
as complete and total
a human being
as they were.

No,
in their eyes,
he was not a full human being,
he was
the blind man.

No name,
no face.

And when his blindness was gone,
they could not recognize the man,
because
their definition of him
was taken away.

But the man himself kept saying
"I am the man."
He knew who he was.
In his own mind
blindness
did not begin to define
the depth of his soul
or the reach of his heart.
He had a face.
He had a name.
He had a heart

as rich with life
as anyone else's.

"I am the man."
"I am the woman."
"I am a human being."

No matter
what our physical state
every single one of us
is made in the image of God,
every single one of us
is a full and complete
human being.

To God
we have
a name,
we have a face.

To know this
is to be liberated
from what anthropologists call
"the social construction of illness."[2]
In the Western world
we tend to think of illness
in almost exclusively
biomedical, physiological terms.
The cause of our malady
is a germ
or a virus
or a malfunctioning organ
or trauma to the body.
There is great truth to this perspective,
and we give thanks to God
for all medical personnel

who carry on through
their science and their art
the ministry of healing.

But this physiological perspective
is not in itself
adequate.
In the story
of Jesus' healing the blind man,
the man's physical state
was not the only issue.
Both Jesus and the blind man
had to deal
with the social construction
of illness and disability.
That social construction
is present in the opening verses
of the story:
"Rabbi, who sinned,
this man or his parents,
that he was born blind?"
According to their social construction of illness,
a disease
or disability
was the result of sin.

The blind man bore not only
the challenge of his blindness
but also the burden
of his society's assumption
that his condition
was a punishment for sin.
He became for them
a man with
no name,
no face,

no identity other than his blindness.
What a horrible burden
to lay on any human being!

We must not think we are above
what these ancient people believed.
We have our own
debilitating social constructions of illness.
For example,
we often deem emotional problems
to be a weakness of character.
Or AIDS may be considered
a punishment for immorality.
Or if someone is deaf
we often couple it with the word "dumb."
In all of these behaviors
we see a tangle of fears
about our own mortality
and frailty.

But Jesus will have none of this.
Jesus stands
opposed
to the rotten belief
that illness or disability
is God's punishment for sin.
God is a God of love,
not a vindictive potentate.
"Neither this man
nor his parents sinned."
Furthermore,
God did not make the man blind
in order to show off God's power.
Many translations
make it sound that way.
They read:

"The man was born blind
so that God's works
might be revealed in him."
But there is another way
to translate the Greek.
It goes like this:
"But that God's power
might be seen at work in him,
we must keep on doing
the works of him who sent me."
Jesus assigns
no one
the blame
for illness and disability.
Jesus with divine wisdom
puts the entire focus
where it belongs:
We must keep on doing
the works of God.
We must keep on healing.
We must keep on
supporting, nurturing,
and tending one another in love.

If we have come here
with a particular illness
or disability
or emotional distress,
or if we have come on behalf
of someone else
Jesus says to us:
"It is not because you
or your beloved
or your parents
or anyone else sinned."

It is not the will of God
that any of God's creatures should suffer.

Tonight we gather
in the Spirit of Christ,
praying
that the two kinds of healing
that took place in the gospel story
may take place here.
We pray
for the mending of bodies,
for the restoration of the mind,
for release from pain.
We pray fervently for these things
trusting that if they do not happen
in this life,
they will happen in a way
beyond all our knowing
in life beyond this life.

And we pray as well
for the healing of our
social construction of illness.
We pray that all human beings
may be freed
of the terrible burden of believing
that God is punishing them
or those they love with illness
or physical disability.
And we pray that those
who would say
such cruel things
will be released from this bitter belief.

Christ is here to say:
"I know that you

are not defined by your physical condition.
I count your tears and hear your sighs.
I know your name.
I see your face.
I understand the yearnings of your hearts
that are too deep for words.
I see in you a full and complete human being
who bears the image of God.
And I love you
with an everlasting love."

Developing Your Own Strategies

I open the Bible and a wind rushes out of its covers, a wind I cannot control, a wind that will not be tamed, a wind that drives me toward visions of what the human community might become by the grace of God. I close the Bible, and the wind keeps blowing.

The wind is the same wind whose force I have encountered outside the Bible, blowing through the images of the converging media and in the lives of those to whom I minister. It is the holy rage I hear in the voices of abused women who are finally allowed to speak up. It is the circular gusts I sense in the hospital where people of faith and conscience have to face ethical questions for which the Bible alone does not give adequate answers. It is the wind that I hear crying in the cries of starving children, the wind that I hear weeping in the weeping of families whose members have been caught in the crossfire of drug lords. It is the storm of hurt that I sense in all who suffer injustice and who find no compassion in church or society. It is the moaning in the human soul of prayers too deep for words. It is the welcome wind that stirs my heart into flame when I hear a preacher who dares to preach that all—all!—human beings are made in the image of God, and there is to be no more killing, no more hatred, no more prejudice, no more religiously sanctioned prejudice. It is the same wind that inspired the biblical writers in their own time and place. It is the power of the Holy Spirit working to capture the human imagination for the purposes of God.

I am not interested in making preachers more imaginative simply in order to make them more entertaining for a multimedia culture, although to be sure, an imaginative preacher will be much more engaging. The imagination of a faithful preacher is an imagination with theological depth.

The constructive theologian, Garrett Green, describes God as the one "who conquers not by force but by 'capturing the imagination' of his fallen human creatures."[1] Television works all the time to capture our imaginations: what it would be like to drive this car, to stay in this hotel chain, to drink this cold beer. The appeal is not simply to our reason, but to what motivates us, what is happening in our hearts.

But since God is also working to capture the human imagination and since our goal in preaching is to participate in winning the human imagination for God, it follows that homiletical methods of cultivating the preacher's imagination are more than ornament or gimmick. If our strategies are worthy of the gospel then they must be rooted in a spirituality that is in touch with the imaginative work of God:

> Proclamation, formulated in terms of the present argument, can be described as an appeal to the imagination of the hearers through the images of scripture. *The preacher's task is to mediate and facilitate that encounter by engaging his or her own imagination, which becomes the link between scripture and congregation.*[2]

In developing our imaginations we are developing a "link" between the congregation and the *logos* of God. Notice: I have changed Green's words; he says *"link between scripture and congregation,"* but I am not willing to leave it at Scripture alone. The way the Bible constantly points beyond itself reveals that to be truly biblical we must extend ourselves beyond the limits of the Bible. Jesus did not say,

"Follow a text," he said, "Follow me." Christianity is not textuality. It is following the risen Savior who would not stay shut up in a grave, and will not stay between the covers of a book, even a holy book. "The two-thousand-year authority of our tradition, erected upon a sealed scriptural testimony, has been welded into a defensive alliance against influxes of fresh illumination."[3]

Yet it is precisely that "fresh illumination" for which our drifting and tormented society cries out. "Back to the Bible" will never fully answer those cries, not only because of the changes in human society and knowledge, but also because the Bible directs us to follow the Holy Spirit, who is not ours to control. The Spirit blows where the Spirit wills.

I am aware that many believers, preachers, and homileticians will consider what I am saying as "dangerous," dangerous to faith, dangerous to a sense of Christian identity. But I would remind them of the dangers of a rigid faith that over the centuries has tortured heretics, burned reformers, blocked the advance of science, justified slavery, and resisted the enfranchisement of women—all on the basis of various readings of the Bible. The true danger is our failure to come to terms with how the human imagination is at work in creating whatever understanding we have of life, including our biblical interpretations. When we ignore the imagination, then we run the risk of promoting a faith that is encrusted with bigotry and dogmatism unworthy of our Savior's name:

> Unlived fantasy and unused imagination burgeon within us and must be put somewhere. We project the unreceived and unexamined images onto our neighbors, near and far. We feel persecuted. We know that there are people out there ready to get us. Those alien to us become our enemies to us. We collectivize them. They become our scapegoats now not in imagination, but in fact, in witch-hunts, flagrant discrimination against "those" of different color, race, religion, sex,

mental capacity, or wealth. . . . The consequences to society of unlived imagination are terrifying.[4]

The answer to the distortions of the human imagination is not to deny or suppress the imagination, but to bring it into relationship with the Holy Spirit, who fills us with world-transforming visions of the reign of God. If we fail to do this, we leave imagination in the hands of the media.

Developing strategies for preaching in a multimedia culture represents, then, a great theological task. No one else can tell you exactly how to do this. The ten strategies in this book will be most fruitful when they set you off to work on your own:

Pray for the Spirit.
Dream.
Experiment.
Test what you preach.
Test it with scripture.
Test it with the congregation.
Test it with your peers.
Test it with your best thought.
Test it with your best feeling.
Test it with your life experience.
Test it with tradition.
Test it against the media.
Test it against the worst of the media.
Test it against the best of the media.
Test it with every gift God has given you.
Modify.
Adapt.
Pray for the Spirit.

If our strategy is faithful to God, then our preaching will come across like the words of a friend who sees more in us than we see in ourselves, who enters our world and helps us claim our best gifts. Christ is such a friend. God says through Christ:

I imagine a world
that is just
and compassionate
and faithful.
I imagine a world at peace.
I imagine all of you living in harmony with creation.
You have that capacity
even though you often fail to see it.
I have made you in my image,
and part of my image
is the gift of imagining
and claiming the world that I intend.

To preach this vision to our multimedia culture is to transform the landscape of the heart and to capture the human imagination for the purposes of God. Surely a goal this great is worthy of all the imaginative energies and gifts our wondrous God has given us.

Notes

In the Path of the Storm

1. Jean Leclercq, O.S.B., *The Love of Learning and the Desire for God*, trans. Catherine Misrahi (New York: Fordham University Press, 1961), p. 317. Cited in Gregor T. Goethals, *The Electronic Golden Calf: Images, Religion, and the Making of Meaning* (Cambridge, Mass.: Cowley Publications, 1990), p. 44.

2. Thomas H. Troeger, *Borrowed Light: Hymn Texts, Prayers, and Poems* (New York: Oxford University Press, 1994), p. 155.

3. M. Jack Suggs, Katharine Doob Sakenfeld, James R. Mueller, *The Oxford Study Bible* (New York: Oxford University Press, 1992), p. 568.

4. Dennis R. MacDonald, "Early Christian Literature," in *The Oxford Study Bible* (New York: Oxford University Press, 1992), p. 117.

5. Ibid., p. 116, emphasis added.

6. Ibid., pp. 113-14.

7. For a readable and useful summary of these see Paul Scott Wilson, *A Concise History of Preaching* (Nashville: Abingdon Press, 1992).

8. Margaret Miles, *Image as Insight: Visual Understanding in Western Christianity and Secular Culture* (Boston: Beacon Press), p. 68.

9. Ibid.

10. Richard Molard quoted in Pierre Babin with Mercedes Iannone, *The New Era in Religious Communication* (Minneapolis: Fortress Press, 1991), p. 25, emphasis added. Babin himself provides a thorough discussion of these issues, and I am drawing on his work in much of what I write.

11. Linda Thomas.

12. James Lull, editor, *World Families Watch Television* (Newbury Park, Calif.: 1988), p. 28.

13. Babin, *New Era*, p. 4.

14. Neil Postman, *Technopoly: The Surrender of Culture to Technology* (New York: Vintage Books, 1993), p. 19.

15. Elizabeth A. Clark, "Biblical Interpretation in the Early Church" in *The Oxford Study Bible* (New York: Oxford University Press, 1992), p. 129.

16. John Taylor, "The Future of Christianity" in *The Oxford Illustrated History of Christianity*, John McManners, ed. (Oxford: Oxford University Press, 1990), p. 641, emphasis added.

17. William Blake, "Auguries of Innocence," in *Selected Poetry and Prose of William Blake* (New York: Modern Library, 1953), p. 90.

18. Babin, *New Era*, p. 83.

19. Averil Cameron, *Christianity and the Rhetoric of Empire: the Development of Christian Discourse* (Berkeley: University of California Press, 1991), p. 20.

20. Ibid., p. 14.

21. Babin, *New Era*, p. 24.

Strategy 1: Assume There Is More to the Story

1. Averil Cameron, *Christianity and the Rhetoric of Empire: the Development of Christian Discourse* (Berkeley: University of California Press, 1991), p. 100.

2. By John of Hildesheim (fourteenth century), as retold by Margaret B. Freeman, *The Story of the Three Kings: Melchior, Balthasar, and Jaspar* (New York: Metropolitan Museum of Art, 1978).

3. Ibid., p. 21.

4. Ibid., p. 17.

5. Ibid., p. 28.

6. James Weldon Johnson, *God's Trombones: Seven Negro Sermons in Verse* (New York: Penguin Books, Viking, 1985), pp. 34-35.

Strategy 3: Play with an Image

1. Gregor T. Goethals, *The Electronic Golden Calf: Images, Religion, and the Making of Meaning* (Cambridge, Mass.: Cowley Publications, 1990), p. 1.

2. Ibid., p. 186. She is drawing here upon the work of Fredric Jameson, "Postmodernism and Consumer Society," in *The Anti-Aesthetic: Essays on Postmodern Culture*, Hal Foster, ed. (Port Townsend, Wash.: Bay Press, 1983), p. 125.

3. This is a rewritten version of a sermon that appeared in *Lectionary Homiletics*, vol. 2, no. 8 (July 1991), pp. 18-19.

Strategy 5: Use a Flashback

1. See strategy 10, "Listen to the Muffled Voices," for further discussion of this topic.

Strategy 6: Reframe a Sacrament

1. The term originated in systems theory, was developed by family therapists, and subsequently found its way into pastoral care. See, e.g., Donald Capps, *Reframing: A New Method in Pastoral Care* (Minneapolis: Fortress Press, 1990). Capps writes, "It [reframing] builds on the idea that a person can break out of limiting perceptions to a broader understanding of human possibilities," pp. 24-25. I am using the concept in this chapter to help people break out of "limiting perceptions" of a sacrament to "a broader understanding" of its meaning for their lives.

Strategy 7: Let a Little Child Lead You

1. Thomas Hood, "I Remember, I Remember," in Helen Gardner, *The New Oxford Book of English Verse* (New York: 1972), p. 619.

Strategy 8: Play a Game

1. Bjorn Krondorfer, "Introduction," in Bjorn Krondorfer, ed., *Body and Bible: Interpreting and Experiencing Biblical Narratives* (Philadelphia: Trinity Press International), p. 2.

2. Cited by Krondorfer, ibid., p. 7.

3. Krondorfer, *Body and Bible*, p. 13.

4. Although I have written all the instructions for the game, the idea is not original with me. Some twenty years ago a minister shared the idea for the game at a conference, and I developed it from there.

5. Write in the number of the household. You can have two to three groups go to the same household.

Strategy 9: Listen to the Muffled Voices

1. See, for example, Philip and Sally Scharper, eds., *The Gospel in Art by the Peasants of Solentiname* (Maryknoll, N.Y.: Orbis Books, 1982); Renita J. Weems, *Just a Sister Away* (San Diego: LuraMedia, 1988); Carol A. Newsom and Sharon H. Ringe, eds., *The Women's Bible Commentary* (Louisville: Westminster/John Knox Press, 1992); Phyllis Trible, *Texts of Terror* (Philadelphia: Fortress Press, 1984). This last was particularly influential in the sermon that follows.

2. Adrian M. S. Piper, "Impartiality, Compassion, and Modal Imagination," *Journal of Ethics* (1991), pp. 732-33.

Strategy 10: Compare Translations

1. Barclay M. Newman and Eugene A. Nida, *A Translator's Handbook on the Gospel of John* (London: United Bible Societies, 1980), p. 299.

2. I am indebted to my colleague, Linda Thomas, an anthropologist and theologian, for introducing and explaining this concept to me.

Developing Your Own Strategies

1. Garrett Green, *Imagining God: Theology and the Religious Imagination* (San Francisco: Harper & Row, 1989), p. 6.

2. Ibid., p. 149, emphasis added.

3. Carl Raschke and Donna Gregory, "Revelation and the Archaeology of the Feminine," in *The Archaeology of the Imagination*, ed. Charles E. Winquist, *Journal of the American Academy of Religious Studies*, vol. 47, no. 2, p. 89.

4. Ann and Barry Ulanov, *The Healing Imagination: The Meeting of Psyche and Soul* (Mahwah, N.J.: Paulist Press, 1991), pp. 43-44.